The Kingfisher Young People's Book of Living Worlds

The Kingfisher Young People's Book of Living Worlds

Clive Gifford • Jerry Cadle

KING*f*ISHER

NEW YORK

Authors Clive Gifford, Jerry Cadle
Consultant Professor Philip Whitfield
Editors Russell Mclean, Jonathan Stroud
Coordinating Editor Sarah Snavely
Designer Mark Bristow
Production Controller Jo Blackmore, Kelly Johnson
Picture Manager Jane Lambert
Picture Researcher Rachael Swann
DTP Manager Nicky Studdart
Indexer Lynn Bresler

KINGFISHER
a Houghton Mifflin Company imprint
215 Park Avenue South
New York, New York 10003
www.houghtonmifflinbooks.com

First published in 2002

2 4 6 8 10 9 7 5 3 1
1TR/0602/TWP/CLSN(CLSN)/150ENSOMA

LIBRARY OF CONGRESS CATALOGING-IN-PUBLICATION
DATA has been applied for.

ISBN 0-7534-5390-8

Printed in Singapore

Contents

Planet Earth

Earth is the only known planet in the universe that supports life. Every sea and continent has its own distinctive life-forms, all adapted to the conditions around them. The millions of different living things that inhabit the planet are found in a narrow layer that extends down into the soil and rocks, and up into the lower parts of Earth's atmosphere. This area is called the biosphere.

Seasons

The power of the Sun provides Earth with the energy it requires to support life. Earth orbits the Sun tilted at an angle, which creates the seasons. When the southern half—or hemisphere—of Earth is tilted toward the Sun, it is the summer in that hemisphere and the winter in the Northern Hemisphere. As the Earth's journey around the Sun continues, the seasons change. Six months later the Northern Hemisphere is tilted toward the Sun, creating summer in the north and winter in the south.

Temperature and climate

How the Sun's rays strike the curved surface of Earth helps determine the temperature of an area. This then affects that area's weather patterns and what can live there. Around the center of Earth—the equator—the temperature is high and does not vary much. This is because the Sun's rays strike from almost directly overhead all year round. Farther away from the equator the Sun's rays strike the surface at a more slanting angle, and their warming effect is decreased. This is why the Poles—the farthest points from the equator—are also the coldest places on Earth. Temperature, height above sea level (or altitude), and distance from the ocean are major influences on a region's climate—the general weather conditions that an area experiences over a long period of time. Rainfall and the strength and types of wind also affect the climate.

Northern
Hemisphere

Equator

Sunlight

Southern
Hemisphere

S

△ As Earth orbits the Sun it rotates on its axis at an angle of 23.5°. This creates the seasons. Pictured above, the Southern Hemisphere is tilted toward the Sun and experiences summer. The Northern Hemisphere experiences winter because it receives less of the Sun's energy. The rays have to travel through more energy-absorbing atmosphere, and they hit Earth's surface at a less direct angle.

▽ Hot, dry deserts—where water is in short supply—exist throughout the world but still support plenty of life. This horned devil lives in a desert in Australia.

▽ This underwater habitat off the west coast of Scotland contains kelp, a type of seaweed that provides shelter for anemones, urchins, and starfish.

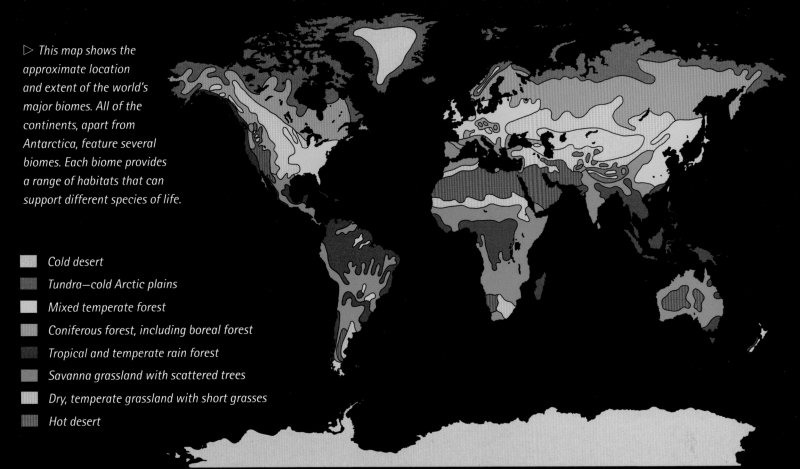

▷ This map shows the approximate location and extent of the world's major biomes. All of the continents, apart from Antarctica, feature several biomes. Each biome provides a range of habitats that can support different species of life.

- ▨ Cold desert
- ▨ Tundra—cold Arctic plains
- ▨ Mixed temperate forest
- ▨ Coniferous forest, including boreal forest
- ▨ Tropical and temperate rain forest
- ▨ Savanna grassland with scattered trees
- ▨ Dry, temperate grassland with short grasses
- ▨ Hot desert

▽ The coldest parts of the world are the two polar regions, where less of the Sun's energy reaches. This icy habitat is in Canada's Northwestern Territories.

▽ Lush bamboo forests in China provide the giant panda with one food source, bamboo shoots. Pandas may die out because they rely too much on one single food.

Biomes

The biosphere provides a large range of different surroundings and living conditions, called environments, for plants and animals. These vary in temperature, moisture, light, and many other factors. The natural home of a plant or animal is called its habitat. Each habitat is a complex, well-balanced system that provides living things with all that they need for survival. A large, general habitat, such as a desert or a tropical rain forest, is called a biome. The largest of all biomes are the oceans, which cover 71 percent of Earth's surface.

◁ The air that surrounds Earth is constantly on the move in the form of air currents and winds. Clouds, formed by millions of droplets of water vapor, are blown around Earth and bring rain and storms to the various regions.

Plants

Plants support all other life on earth. They are **autotrophs**, which means that they can survive on direct energy sources, such as sunlight. They also take nutrients from soil, rocks, and water. The types of plants growing in an area often define what kind of biome it is and what else can survive there because they offer food, homes, and shelter for many animals. Plants cannot move, but some of their parts are designed for travel. This means they can reproduce with other plants and then scatter their seeds, which will grow into the next generation of plants.

Ingredients of life

Plants need four basic things to grow and live: water, carbon dioxide, mineral salts, and light. Water and minerals are drawn up through a plant's roots, its leaves take in carbon dioxide from the air, and light is absorbed directly from the sun. Water, carbon dioxide, and light are used by plants to manufacture their own food in a process called photosynthesis. The energy from sunlight is used to convert the water and carbon dioxide into sugars, which act as a plant's food. Photosynthesis also plays a vital role in recycling air. It produces a waste product called oxygen—a type of gas most animals need to breathe in order to survive.

▽ *Plants that grow in soil that lacks nutrients have evolved to obtain them from elsewhere. This sundew is a meat-eating plant. It traps and digests insects to get mineral nutrients.*

Nutrients

Most plants need extra nutrients besides those that they make themselves during photosynthesis. These include minerals, such as nitrogen and magnesium, which they get in water from the soil. Minerals in the soil are usually plentiful, unless the same crop has been grown intensively for many years in a row. Farmers need to rotate their crops by growing plants such as lupins and clover in between their main crops. These plants enrich the soil by producing more nitrogen than they use.

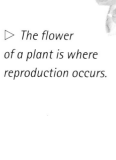

▷ *The flower of a plant is where reproduction occurs.*

▷ *Carbon dioxide passes into a plant through tiny pores, or holes, called stomata in the leaf's surface.*

▷ *Chlorophyll, a chemical that gives plants their green color, is stored in the leaves in packages called chloroplasts. Photosynthesis occurs in the chloroplasts.*

▷ *Water and the sugary sap created by photosynthesis are carried throughout a plant by veins in the stem and leaves.*

▷ *Water is taken in through the root system of a plant.*

Flowers

Flowering plants produce male and female sex cells in different parts of their flowers. The flower's female cells lie at the base of a stalk called the style. Pollen is the male part of the flower. It grows on another stalk called the stamen and needs to reach the female sex cells of another plant in order for reproduction to take place. Grasses and many other plants rely on the wind to spread their pollen, while plants with large flowers use the flowers to attract insects and other creatures. These animals carry sticky pollen on their bodies from one plant's flowers to another.

◁ *Flowers are often brightly colored to attract pollen carriers. Many contain sweet, sticky nectar, which provides food for birds, bats, and insects, such as this bee.*

▽ *The seeds of dandelions are shaped like tiny parachutes so that they can be carried by the wind. A strong wind can blow the seeds several miles away from the parent plant.*

Seeds and spores

Seeds develop after a plant has been pollinated. They are often encased in a protective coating to form nuts, fruit, or berries. If the coating is nutritious, it will be eaten by animals, which disperse the seeds in their droppings. Some seeds, such as winged sycamore seeds or dandelion parachutes, are shaped to catch the wind. Others are covered in small hooks that attach to an animal's fur. Ferns, mosses, and liverworts don't create seeds at all. Instead they have tiny spores that disperse in the wind.

Germination

Germination is the process by which a seed starts to grow into a plant. For a seed to germinate it must be resting in suitable soil with sufficient light and water. Seeds contain a food supply to sustain the seedling until it has grown enough to produce its own food through photosynthesis.

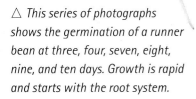

△ *This series of photographs shows the germination of a runner bean at three, four, seven, eight, nine, and ten days. Growth is rapid and starts with the root system.*

Our living planet

Animals

Like plants, animals can grow, sense changes in their environment, and reproduce to make a new generation of young. Animals, however, cannot photosynthesize in order to create their own food from sunlight, water, and gases. They are heterotrophs, which means they must eat something that is or was alive in order to refuel themselves. Most animals are equipped with muscles or other structures that allow them to move around. They also need to take in oxygen through respiration, or breathing.

△ Supported by water, which has a similar density to their bodies, this school of mullets swim by simply moving their tails back and forth. On land animals use more energy and require stronger muscles, skeletons, and hearts to move.

Structure and movement

Animals whose bodies are supported by a backbone are called vertebrates. Invertebrates are animals without a backbone. Vertebrates include mammals, birds, reptiles, and fish. They all have an internal skeleton made of bone, or in the case of sharks a tough substance called cartilage. Invertebrates, such as worms, insects, crustaceans, spiders, and jellyfish, are far more common but are usually smaller and less complex animals. Most animals have muscles to power their movement—from the heart pumping blood around the body to the movement of legs, wings, or fins that propels an animal around.

▽ One of the largest predators on land is the female lion, or lioness, here seen stalking a herd of springbok antelope in the grasslands of southern Africa.

△ This grass snake shows great agility, plunging underwater and catching a fish.

Feeding

Most animals, from small insects to enormous elephants, are herbivores—they eat plant matter. Others are meat eaters, called carnivores. Some animals, such as worms, bears, humans, and some birds, are omnivores—able to eat both animals and plants. Food has to be broken down, or digested, for its nutrients to be absorbed. This is usually done inside an animal's body with the help of chemicals called enzymes. Carnivores have developed amazing ways of catching prey—they use webs and traps, work in teams, or rely on sheer speed or power. As protection from carnivores many animals have evolved defenses such as armor and stingers. Others hide, use camouflage, or live together in large groups to keep from being attacked.

▷ Ospreys hunt for fish by hovering over the water and then diving with their wings swept back. At the last moment they thrust their talons forward to pluck the fish from below the water's surface. Adult ospreys are successful about once every four dives.

Senses

Animals need senses to find food, shelter, and others of the same species, as well as to avoid danger. Just like humans, most animals are equipped with five senses: sound, smell, touch, taste, and sight. In many cases creatures have one or two senses that are more highly developed than the others. For example, high-flying turkey vultures have powerful long-distance sight and smell, enabling them to detect dead animals while flying hundreds of feet above the ground. Many creatures have one poorly-developed sense or may be missing a sense entirely, which is compensated by other, more sensitive ones. Nocturnal animals—which feed and are most active at night—often have poor vision but enhanced senses of smell, hearing, and touch.

◁ A spider uses sensitive hairs on its body as touch and taste receptors. The hairs also sense air currents and humidity. Most spiders have eight eyes. This jumping spider has four eyes on the front of its head and four on the top.

Communication

Animals communicate for many reasons—from calling a lost baby or attracting a mate to sounding the alarm about an approaching predator. They communicate in a great variety of ways. Sound is used by animals on land, sea, and air. Birdsong often marks a bird's territory or keeps it in touch with the rest of its flock. The haunting and complex "songs" of the humpback whale can be heard by another humpback hundreds of miles away. Many mammals use a combination of body language and sounds to communicate a threat or show they are ready to mate. Bees perform a dance to let others know the location of a food source. Scents and smells are very important to many creatures, from ants to big cats, to help them find food and communicate with others.

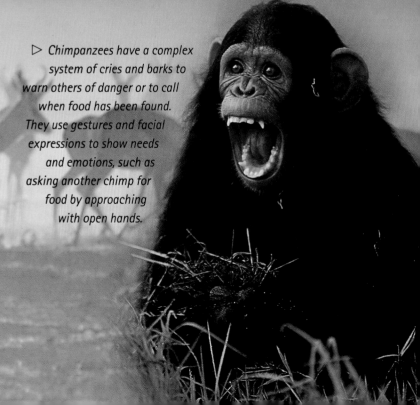

▷ Chimpanzees have a complex system of cries and barks to warn others of danger or to call when food has been found. They use gestures and facial expressions to show needs and emotions, such as asking another chimp for food by approaching with open hands.

Our living planet

Ecosystems

An ecosystem is a complicated system of relationships between plants, animals, and the environment and climate in which they live. Ecosystems are communities of living things and their surroundings and can be large—a complete coral reef, for example—or small, such as a single rotting tree in a woodland. The study of the relationships between different animals, plants, and their environment is called ecology.

Food chains and webs

All living things in an ecosystem are linked by the transfer of energy between the many species that live there. The links can be shown in diagrams known as food chains and food webs. Food chains show the transfer of energy from plants to different animals. Plants, which convert energy from sunlight into food, are known as primary producers. Animals that eat plants and live directly off the food stored in them are called primary consumers. Secondary consumers are animals that eat primary consumers, while tertiary consumers are those that eat secondary consumers. Many creatures eat a range of plants and animals, both producers and consumers. Food webs try to reflect this complexity by mapping the interlinked collection of food chains in an ecosystem.

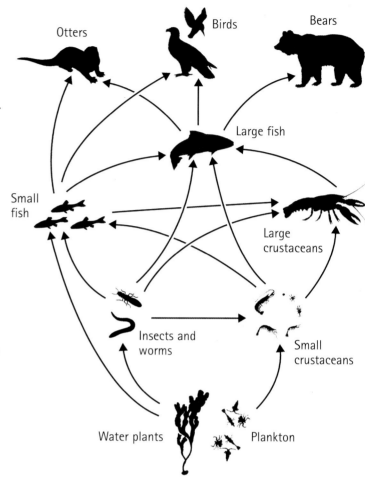

△ This food web shows a simplified view of energy transfer in a river ecosystem. The arrows travel from the food source to the animal consuming it. Top predators, such as the bear, are not eaten by any other animal.

△ The niche of the red fox is that of a predator in a forest fringe habitat. It eats small mammals, insects, and fruit. Flies and mosquitoes feed on the fox's blood, and the scraps of meat it leaves behind after a kill are food for scavengers and decomposers.

Evolution and niches

Since life began on earth around 3.5 billion years ago, millions of different species have changed and developed. This process of long-term change is called evolution. Many scientists believe that evolution works using a process called natural selection. Natural selection is based on the inherited differences between members of the same species. Those organisms with differences that let them adapt best to their environment are more likely to survive and pass on those differences to the next generation. Over many generations organisms evolve into many different forms, which find niches in even the busiest and most crowded ecosystems. A living thing's ecological niche is its unique way of life within an ecosystem. It includes both the animal or plant's physical habitat and how it has adapted to life in that habitat.

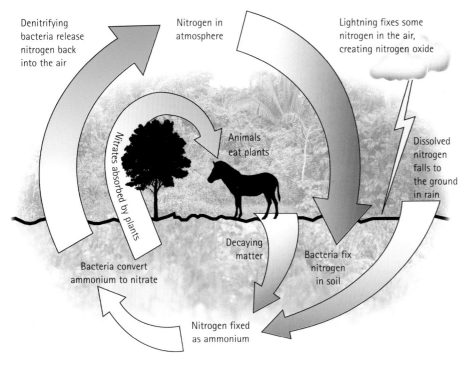

Denitrifying bacteria release nitrogen back into the air

Nitrogen in atmosphere

Lightning fixes some nitrogen in the air, creating nitrogen oxide

Nitrates absorbed by plants

Animals eat plants

Dissolved nitrogen falls to the ground in rain

Bacteria convert ammonium to nitrate

Decaying matter

Bacteria fix nitrogen in soil

Nitrogen fixed as ammonium

△ All living things need nitrogen to grow. Approximately 78 percent of air consists of nitrogen, but because it is an unreactive gas, plants and animals cannot use it. So nitrogen has to be fixed—changed into soluble nitrates that plants can use—by bacteria. Bacteria also complete the cycle by releasing nitrogen back into the atmosphere.

Cycles and recycling

For life to continue on earth the resources used by living things need to be recycled so that they are not all used up. Ecosystems rely on a series of cycles in which water, oxygen, nitrogen, carbon, and minerals are generated, used, and recycled. The food and nutrients that living things require are also recycled. When plants or animals die, their bodies form the diet for organisms such as bacteria, fungi, worms, and slugs. These are known as decomposers. They break down dead animal and plant matter and release chemicals into the air, water, and soil. The nutrients put back into the soil by decomposers are vital because the primary producers—the plants— use them to grow and flourish.

▷ Fungi, such as these fairies' bonnets, are major decomposers of dead plant matter. Fairies' bonnets grow in clusters out of rotten wood.

◁ Anemone fish and sea anemones have a relationship from which both benefit. Anemone fish ward off other fish that prey on sea anemones. In return, they are able to hide from predators in the stinging tentacles of the sea anemone without being harmed.

▷ This deer tick is a parasite, feeding on an animal's blood. Ticks can transmit Lyme disease as they eat, which affects the skin, heart, and nervous system of the host animal.

Symbiosis

Symbiosis is a close relationship between the individuals of two or more species. When both species benefit, it is known as mutualism. For example, squirrels obtain food from an oak tree in the form of acorns. In return, they disperse the acorns over a wide area. Commensalism is when one species benefits while the other is unaffected. Species of mites live on a sloth, eating the algae in its fur but making no difference to the sloth. Parasitism is when one species benefits while harming the other. For example, the tick is a parasite that lives by sucking another animal's blood. As it feeds the tick may transmit diseases to its host.

Seas and oceans

Life on earth began in the water, and today water covers nearly three quarters of the planet's surface. There are five oceans—the Pacific, the Atlantic, the Indian, the Antarctic, and the Arctic. Smaller bodies of water, such as the Mediterranean and the Caribbean, are called seas. The waters contain many different habitats—from the dark and hostile ocean depths to the teeming coral reefs— and support a huge variety of life. Seas and oceans have a level of species diversity as high as in the rain forests.

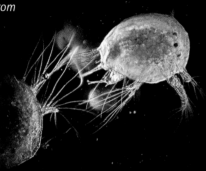

▷ Plankton, such as these examples from the waters around Great Britain, are divided into animal plankton and plant plankton. Plant plankton produce almost 70 percent of the world's oxygen.

▽ Anglerfish are named after an extension of their dorsal fin that can be wiggled like a fishing lure to attract prey. Usually living in water over 50 ft. (15m) deep, anglerfish have been known to leave the seabed and attack seabirds on the water's surface.

Plankton

Food chains in seas and oceans start with primary producers called plant plankton or phytoplankton. They live close to the water's surface in order to absorb sunlight. They use the light to make food through photosynthesis. Plankton also exist in animal form called zooplankton. These cannot photosynthesize and instead feed off of other animal plankton or plant plankton. Unlike phytoplankton, many zooplankton can swim rather than merely drift in the water. The different types of plankton form the crucial first stage of the marine food chain, which supports sea plants, crustaceans, fish, and water mammals, such as seals.

◁ This giant Pacific octopus has two rows of suckers on each of its arms to catch prey, such as this cabizon fish. The octopus kills the prey with its beak and bites it into pieces.

Fish

Fish breathe by swallowing water and passing it over their gills—feathery tissues lined with blood vessels that absorb oxygen from the water. Most fish—over 20,000 species—are bony. Many bony fish, such as mackerel and herring, are streamlined and live in large schools near the water's surface. They are called pelagic fish. Other bony fish, such as the sole and the halibut, are flattened and live on the seabed. They are known as demersal fish. A bony fish has a gas-filled sac inside its body called a swim bladder that enables it to float. About 600 species of fish have no bones, instead they have a skeleton made of tough cartilage. These cartilaginous fish, such as sharks, tend to sink unless they keep swimming.

▷ *Deep-sea tube worms grow up to 10 ft. (3m) long. Their tail ends are attached to the ocean floor. The red plumes at the top contain blood, which carries hydrogen sulfide from deep-sea vents to the bacteria inside their bodies.*

◁ *Manta rays are the largest species of rays, averaging 22 ft. (6.7m) in width. They eat plankton, tiny fish, and small crustaceans. A school of fish swims beneath this ray for protection.*

Into the deep

Most marine life exists in the top 330 ft. (100m) of water, where light and plankton are plentiful. Yet the average ocean depth is 12,140 ft. (3,700m). At such great depths there is no light, little food, and extreme pressure. The animals that live there are adapted to the extreme conditions, and many rely on food falling down from the water above. Many deep-water animals produce their own light in order to communicate, catch prey, or deter predators. This light, known as bioluminescence, is often generated by bacteria living inside the animals.

Black smokers

In 1977 new forms of life were discovered in the ocean depths. They were found around rocky chimneys, called black smokers, on the seabed. Rocks beneath earth's crust heat water, which seeps down through cracks in the seabed, to temperatures of 752°F (400°C). The water blasts back up to the sea floor, carrying minerals from the crust that are deposited to form chimneys. Bacteria thrive in the sulfur-rich waters of these hot spots and provide the crucial first stage in a food web that supports blind white crabs, sea anemones more than 3 ft. (1m) wide, giant clams, and tube worms.

▷ *Giant clams cluster around a deep-sea vent in the ocean floor, 8,530 ft. (2,600m) below sea level. Little is known about their life cycle, but it is believed that, like tube worms, they rely on bacteria to break down the nutrients they eat.*

Coral reefs

In the kaleidoscopic world of the coral reef there is a greater variety of life than anywhere else in the sea. Over one third of all the world's fish species live there. Many animals, including sea slugs, starfish, and small fish, come to eat the coral, and they then attract predators, such as sharks and barracuda. With so many predators around, some of the reef creatures are camouflaged, but most have bright displays to warn that they are poisonous or to help them find a mate, making the reef a tapestry of different colors.

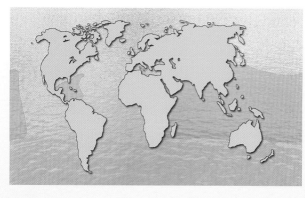

△ Reefs grow only under certain conditions. They need strong sunlight and water temperatures of 68°F (20°C) or above, which can usually only be found in tropical waters up to 131 ft. (40m) deep. The orange areas on this map show the regions where reefs can grow.

How reefs are formed

Coral is made by large colonies of small creatures called polyps. Ranging in size from one tenth of a centimeter to one centimeter, the individual polyps consist of a central mouth and stomach surrounded by a ring of plankton-catching tentacles. The polyps grow hard external skeletons for protection, and when they die, these remain as a stony mass on the seabed. A coral reef gradually builds up as successive generations of polyps live on top of the growing pile of skeletons of their predecessors. It is a very slow process, with the reefs growing no more than a few centimeters every year. Many are thousands of years old.

△ A polyp's hard outer skeleton helps protect it from predators, while its tentacles trap passing plankton. The corals' bright colors are caused by algae growing within their tissues. In return for a place to live, the algae provide the corals with some of the food they make for themselves during photosynthesis.

▽ The living surface of the reef is formed of many different coral species, including the brain coral (below center). Nooks and crannies within the layers of dead and living coral create perfect lairs for predators like this moray eel.

The Great Barrier Reef

The largest reef is the Great Barrier Reef, which lies off the northeast coast of Australia. It stretches for 1,240 mi. (2,000km), and is home to over 1,500 species of fish. Big enough to be seen from space, the Great Barrier Reef has parts that are over two million years old—the oldest structure made by living organisms. Today the Great Barrier Reef is threatened by a coral-eating starfish called the crown-of-thorns. Since the 1970s, a plague of crown-of-thorns has swept the reef, devouring the coral and leaving vast regions barren and empty.

A threatened future

More than 90 percent of coral reefs are being damaged in some way. Heavy tropical storms break up the coral, and so do fishermen when they drag their nets. Coral can be poisoned by pollution from shipping and other industries, and the algae living within the coral are killed if the sea temperature changes. As global warming increases the algae in more and more coral will be destroyed, bleaching them of color and depriving them of a valuable food source.

▷ *The crown-of-thorns starfish multiplied rapidly when its natural predators, large marine snails, were collected by humans. The sale of the snail shells has now been banned in an effort to halt the starfish plague.*

△ *Parrot fish are a natural predator of coral, although they do not cause serious damage. They eat the polyps and the algae in them, using special, chisel-shaped teeth that grind away the coral's protective skeleton.*

▽ *Many of the animals that thrive on a coral reef are among the oldest creatures on earth. Corals, sponges, and starfish have existed together for 500 million years—100 million years longer than the fish that now swim past them.*

▽ *Schools of fish browse the gentle, nutrient-rich waters of the reef. Its mazelike structure provides them with some protection from predators, such as the reef shark, which patrols the open waters of the reef at night.*

Coasts and wetlands

Coastlines are found on every continent. Ranging from towering cliffs and jagged rocks to gravel or sand beaches, they are unusual habitats that alternate between wet and dry. The animals that live there have to adapt to conditions both underwater and in the drying sun in order to survive. The majority of coastal life also has to deal with the problem of pounding waves. Yet for the plants and animals that manage to exist there the coastal environment can be ideal for growth, with plenty of sunlight, water, and mineral salts from the sea.

△ A mixture of different seaweeds in a tidal pool on the French coast.

Intertidal zone

The area where the sea meets the land is called the intertidal zone. Sometimes the zone is submerged under saltwater, at other times it is exposed to the air as the tides come in and go out. On rocky coasts the intertidal zone is divided into three habitats. At the top, where only the highest tides reach, less life exists—mainly algae and mollusks. The areas always covered by high tide support a greater range of animals, including small fish, plant-eating snails, and crabs. The bottom of the intertidal zone is exposed only during the lowest tides. Many fish, seaweeds, sea anemones, starfish, and sea urchins are found here. On sandier shores the intertidal zone is not so strictly divided. Mud and sand is always on the move, which makes it hard for algae or plants to settle in. Worms, clams, crustaceans, crabs, and shorebirds occupy this area.

▽ The rocky Farne Islands provide homes for large colonies of guillemots, puffins, and terns.

△ Low tide attracts predators, particularly seabirds such as these oystercatchers. They are drawn by the number of small animals hidden just below the sand's surface.

◁ Sea otters are one of the few animals to use tools. This sea otter is opening a shell by smashing it against a rock balanced on its belly.

Avoiding exposure

When the tide starts to go out, many coastal animals hide to avoid drying out in the sun. Wet, heavy seaweed or damp crevices in rocks are a retreat for shore-dwelling crabs. Many animals with shells simply burrow into the sand, emerging when the water returns. Others, such as cockles and razor shells, stay buried and extend a tube called a feeding siphon to pull in food-rich water. For animals that are anchored to the rocks, burying themselves is not an option. The sea anemone, for example, withdraws its tentacles and covers itself with a protective, jellylike mucus. This prevents it from drying out and dying.

◁ A sea anemone has tentacles that trap, sting, and draw prey, such as this fish, to its central mouth.

▽ Mudskippers are fish found in wetlands and mangrove swamps. They can live out of water, using their strong pectoral fins to skip along.

Wetlands

Wetlands are swampy areas where water lies on the land in pools or where plants have grown out into open water to form marshes or swamps. The still water supports a huge range of aquatic plants and animals. Wetlands often have the highest species diversity of all ecosystems. They are home to many species of amphibians, reptiles, and birds, such as ducks and waders. Estuaries are areas where freshwater streams or rivers merge with saltwater from the ocean. Worms, oysters, crabs, waterfowl, algae, seaweeds, marsh grasses, and (in the tropics) mangrove trees, can all be found in estuaries.

▽ The cliffs at Hunstanton on Great Britain's East Anglian coast are formed of brown carstone topped with white chalk. The cliffs have been heavily eroded, forming a stony shoreline.

Rivers and lakes

When rain falls on high ground, some of the water soaks into the soil or seeps between cracks in the rocks. Water that remains on the surface creates a stream because it is drawn by gravity down to sea level. Streams join together to become rivers. These huge bodies of moving water carve and erode rocks and land, creating valleys and gorges. Lakes form where water collects and is not able to drain away. Both rivers and lakes are home to a wide range of plants and animals.

△ Some insects have adapted to life underwater in lakes and ponds. The water boatman stores air beneath its wings, so it can stay submerged for long periods of time as it feeds on plants.

The river ecosystem

A river offers more than one habitat. Different living things are found on the riverbed, at the water's surface, and at the water's edge. Plant life along the edge of the river is a home and a food source for many animals. Rivers also change along their length—they flow fast in their early stages and meander slowly as they empty into the sea. In fast-flowing sections the fish are very strong swimmers, and some insects have developed ways of coping with the rushing water. Caddisworms, for example, build a case of sticks and sand to weigh themselves down. Many animals spend only a part of their lives in rivers. Salmon and trout are born and die in rivers, but in between they live at sea. Amphibians such as toads and frogs develop in freshwater as larvae and tadpoles but spend much of their adult lives on land.

◁ Kingfishers feed on small fish, such as this stickleback. They dive into the water to catch their prey, and then they swallow it head first. Kingfishers live in lowland areas around clear, slow-moving rivers.

▷ Rainbow trout are migratory fish, starting and ending their lives in rivers. They are strong enough to swim against the current of a fast-flowing river and even leap upstream.

The Amazon

The Amazon River begins in the snow-capped Andes Mountain, in South America, and then it winds through the Amazon basin before reaching the Atlantic Ocean. At 4,040 mi. (6,500km) long it is slightly shorter than the Nile River, but the 1,000 tributaries that run into the Amazon fill it with more water than any other river. One fifth of the freshwater that enters the sea every year comes from the Amazon River.

△ The huge leaves of the Amazon water lily float on the water's surface. Each plant can grow as many as 50 leaves.

▽ The Amazon River is home to one of the world's largest and heaviest snakes—the anaconda. Anacondas lie in wait for prey such as turtles, capybara (the world's largest rodent), and iguanas. They kill by suffocating their prey as they wrap their coils around the victim and squeeze out its breath.

Giant wildlife

The Amazon River's food-rich habitats have allowed giant versions of some animals and plants to evolve. The world's largest otter, the giant otter, can grow up to 8 ft. (2.5m) long. It emerges from its den on the riverbank to hunt for fish and crabs during the day. The huge Amazon water lily anchors its roots in the mud of the riverbed and grows quickly. Each of its leaves can grow to 6 ft. (1.8m) across.

▽ The Cononaco River winds through the Yasuni National Park in Ecuador, South America. Surrounded by lush rain forests, the river is one of the homes of the Amazon River dolphin.

▽ Lakes make up a very small percentage of all the freshwater on earth, but they are rich habitats for life. This lake in Rwanda has formed in the crater of an extinct volcano.

Lakes

Lakes form in different ways. Many, such as the five Great Lakes, were carved out by glaciers during past ice ages. Others occur because of movement of earth's plates or develop in the craters of extinct volcanoes. The action of humans and animals, such as beavers, can also create lakes. Shallow lakes and ponds are often rich in nutrients and wildlife. Plankton—the microscopic organisms that float in water—are food for small insects and crustaceans. Aquatic plants are vital for the health of most lakes. They provide food and a place to live and breed for lake animals, as well as releasing oxygen into the water.

⚫ People and water

Water is the most precious resource on earth.
It is essential for life and is the habitat for many
of the world's living things. People rely on water
for many reasons, not just for drinking, to survive—
they hunt salt- and freshwater animals for food,
they use water in manufacturing, and they channel
it to irrigate agricultural fields and provide power.
People also damage sea- and freshwater environments
through pollution and by overusing their contents.

△ Viewed from space,
the Nile River winds through
Egypt, providing a ribbon
of fertile land on either side
of its banks. This fertile zone
supports industry, agriculture,
and over 95 percent of Egypt's
human population.

Tourism

Tourism is one of the world's biggest and fastest-growing industries.
Coastal areas are often the target of this trillion-dollar business. Unspoiled coastal
regions on every continent except Antarctica have been developed into high-rise
resorts, often with little thought to the ecological consequences. Natural wetlands,
lagoons, and coastline habitats are cleared or drained to make way for hotels and
roads. Tourist facilities may pump unclean wastewater into the sea, creating further
damage. The massive increase in tourist numbers can destroy delicate habitats such
as coral reefs, while the high demand for local foods can lead to a decline
in the number of shellfish and fish.

◁ Cancún, in Mexico, took
just 20 years to develop into
a resort with 1.5 million
visitors every year. Around
148,200 acres (60,000ha)
of rain forest were cleared,
and parts of Cancún's lagoon
were destroyed or contaminated
—affecting habitats for native
plants, marine turtles, fish,
and other animals.

Pollution

Many substances dissolve easily in water, making it highly vulnerable to pollution from many sources—domestic sewage, dumped industrial chemicals, and agricultural pesticides that can be washed from the soil into streams and rivers. Oil spills have been especially devastating to marine and coastal habitats, injuring and killing an abundance of marine life. The *Exxon Valdez* supertanker spilled over 11 million gallons (50 million *l*) of crude oil onto the coast of Alaska in 1989. Some of the species and the fishing communities living there still have not recovered fully.

△ *Oil slicks clog the fur of animals and the feathers of birds, such as this kittiwake. Oil can block the gills of fish, preventing them from breathing, and oil poisons animals that accidentally swallow it.*

Fishing

Fish have been a primary source of food for people in coastal areas and on islands for thousands of years. Modern sea fishing uses giant trawlers to haul in millions of tons of fish every year at a rate that nature cannot keep up with. Many species, such as cod, haddock, and certain shellfish, have been overfished. In some places fish populations will recover only if fishing is limited by quotas or even halted altogether. At some fishing grounds species have been overfished, causing local extinction. The animals that rely on these species for food have also gone into decline, damaging the entire marine ecosystem. Modern fishing can also be extremely wasteful, with many unwanted sea creatures caught and killed in nets, including turtles, dolphins, diving seabirds, and certain species of fish.

△ *These fishermen are hauling in a catch of herring. Of the world's 13 million fishermen, one million crew the 30,000 large fishing vessels that catch half of the world's fish.*

▽ *Hydroelectric power plants need large dams, such as the Glen Canyon dam on the Colorado River, to hold back a giant reservoir of water. Building dams may cause rivers to be diverted and valleys flooded, destroying habitats and many animals.*

Water power

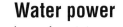

Moving water can be exploited to produce electricity. A hydroelectric power plant uses a large dam to create a reservoir of water and then lets some surge through a tunnel to machines called turbines. The turbines are turned by the falling water, powering generators that create electricity. Although dams offer a renewable source of energy, they are expensive to build and can seriously disrupt local ecosystems. Another form of water power harnesses the energy in tides. Tidal barriers stretch across part of a shoreline or estuary, and their turbines are turned by the tide flowing in and out. The barriers are expensive to build, threaten certain habitats, and prevent fish, like salmon, from swimming up estuaries.

23

Rain forests

Rain forests are the most complex and productive biomes on earth. They consist of huge trees growing closely together, interlocking, and rising up to 130 ft. (40m) above the ground. Rain forests thrive on sunlight and very heavy rain—between 80–400 in. (200–1,000cm) of rainfall every year. The rain produces lush plant growth, which in turn supports an enormous number of animals. Although rain forests make up under ten percent of earth's land surface, scientists estimate that they are home to as much as 90 percent of the world's animal and plant species.

▷ The temperate rain forests on the west coast of New Zealand receive up to 275 in. (700cm) of rainfall every year. The forests bustle with plant and animal life.

△ Rain forests are home to huge numbers of bird species, such as these scarlet ibises in Venezuela. In the rain forests of Costa Rica, for example, there are 845 different bird species, as well as 205 kinds of mammals and more than 10,000 varieties of plants.

Where are rain forests?

Rain forests are divided into two types: tropical and temperate. Tropical rain forests are hot (at least 60–77°F/ 20–25°C) and are found close to the equator. Over 50 percent of all tropical rain forests are in Latin America. Southeast Asia, the Pacific Islands, and West and central Africa are home to approximately 43 percent. Temperate rain forests are also wet but have a milder climate. They are found farther from the equator, near the coast, and once covered large parts of Scotland, Iceland, Norway, and Ireland. Today Chile, New Zealand, and the Pacific Coast are homes to the largest remaining temperate rain forests.

Rain forest layers

Rain forests are made up of four basic layers, or strata: the forest floor, the understory, the canopy, and the emergent layer. The plants and animals that live in each layer are specifically adapted to life there. Each layer has its own particular microclimate according to the level of light and water it receives. The canopy is a rain forest's powerhouse—it receives up to 90 percent of all sunlight that falls on the rain forest. Here photosynthesis is most productive, producing rapid plant growth. For example, 2.5 acres (1ha) of tropical rain forest produces more than 60 tons of new plant growth every year, twice as much as a temperate oak forest.

131 ft. (40m)

▷ The emergents are the tallest trees, scattered through the rain forest. Their tops poke out above the canopy.

98 ft. (30m)

▷ The canopy comprises the interlocking tops of the main forest trees. The majority of rain forest animals live here.

66 ft. (20m)

▷ The understory is made up of small trees, shrubs, bushes, ferns, and vines that can survive in shady conditions.

33 ft. (10m)

▷ The forest floor is damp, dark, and still as the plants above protect it from the winds. Humidity levels are 90 percent or above.

◁ Climbing plants, such as this vine in Peru, are common in rain forests. They snake up and around tree trunks, tying many trees together so that if one falls, many fall with it.

Rain forests and the world's weather

Rain forests have a major impact on the well-being of the entire planet. As well as generating huge amounts of oxygen through photosynthesis, rain forests also help maintain global rain and weather patterns. The dense plant foliage acts like a giant sponge, soaking up large quantities of falling rain before it can seep away. Much of the water returns to the air as water vapor given off by leaves. The vapor condenses to form rain clouds both over the forest and on land that is far away.

▽ An epipyhte is a type of hanging plant. By growing on the branches of canopy trees they receive sunlight without having to grow up from the forest floor.

◁ Clouds form quickly above the dense, green canopy of a tropical rain forest in Venezuela. Without rain forests many areas of the world would be affected by droughts.

The forest floor

Far below the rain forest canopy lies the dark world of the forest floor. Only two percent of the light that hits the uppermost branches reaches the ground, so few plants are able to grow among the fungi and twisting roots that cover its surface. Yet the leaf litter around the roots teems with life. Insects—from giant beetles to poisonous centipedes—are everywhere, and it is so wet that frogs, crabs, and even fish are able to flourish in the gloom.

Releasing the nutrients

Rain forest soil is very poor. It contains few nutrients, and what little it does have is easily washed away by the rains that swamp the forests. The main source of nutrition for the trees is the layer of leaf litter and dead plant and animal debris that covers the forest floor. Here huge numbers of decomposers, such as bacteria, fungi, and insects, break down the litter into nutrients. These are then taken in by the trees through their huge networks of roots. Special fungi called mycorrhizae cover the root tips and work with the trees, helping them absorb the precious nutrients before they are washed away.

▽ *Many of the forest trees have huge buttress roots to prop them up in the thin soil. Around them small seedlings wait in suspended animation for a hole to appear in the canopy above. They will then grow rapidly, racing each other to fill the gap.*

▽▷ The lush conditions of the forest allow many species to grow to a giant size. Carnivorous centipedes (right) can reach 11 in. (28cm) long. Land crabs (below) live in the moist leaf litter, as well as in the water that collects at the bottom of bromeliad plants.

Down in the litter

The leaf litter is so damp and humid that creatures normally found in aquatic habitats live here. Frogs and land crabs scurry through the leaves. The warm, wet conditions allow invertebrates to grow to gigantic sizes. Giant centipedes hunt at night for prey that includes rodents and snakes, and huge maggots of the world's largest beetle, the Goliath beetle, pupate in the rotting leaves.

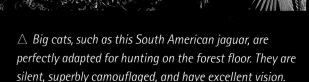

△ *Big cats, such as this South American jaguar, are perfectly adapted for hunting on the forest floor. They are silent, superbly camouflaged, and have excellent vision.*

A solitary life

The vegetation of the forest floor is too sparse to support large herds of big herbivores. Those that live here tend to be solitary creatures. Tiny deer and large rodents, such as the agoutis and pacas, forage for smaller plants in the forests of South America. Taller plants are reached by animals such as the tapir, forest rhino, and, in Africa, the okapi. Their predators— mostly the big cats—are also very few in number.

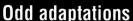

▷ *The okapi is a relative of the giraffe. This extremely shy creature was first discovered in the African rain forest in 1901.*

Odd adaptations

To adapt to the extreme lack of light some forest floor plants, such as rafflesia, tap into the trunks of trees whose leaves reach into the light of the canopy and steal their food. Others have giant leaves or systems that act like lenses in their foliage to make the most of the dim light. Nearly all have special drip tips on their leaves to drain off the constant moisture and prevent them from getting moldy.

◁ *Rafflesia is a parasitic plant that steals the food and water supplies of the vines that grow on the trees above it. Its huge flower—at 3 ft. (1m) wide, the largest in the world—smells like rotting flesh. This attracts flies, which spread its pollen.*

The canopy

The majority of life in a rain forest is found in its canopy, high above the ground. Unlike the forest floor, the canopy basks in sunlight—ideal for rapid plant growth. Leaves, flowers, fruits, nuts, and seeds are valuable food sources for a large variety of animals—from butterflies, ants, and other insects to frogs, lizards, and larger creatures such as fruit-eating monkeys. Many of these have evolved and adapted to life in the canopy, finding ways to move, build homes, feed, and reproduce high above the ground.

▷ The canopy food web involves thousands of different living things. The lush plant life provides a rich food source for insects and some birds, monkeys, and mammals. These animals are then food for predators, such as snakes and large birds of prey.

△ Rain forest canopies support many small, aquatic microcommunities. These tadpoles are living in a pool of water that has formed in the leaves of a bromeliad, a type of epiphyte.

Eagles

Snakes

Birds

Bats

Frogs

Sloths

Monkeys

Insects

Squirrels

Leaves

▽ A northern blossom bat feeds on a banksia flower in Australia. Bats are major pollinators of flowering plants.

Fruits

PLANTS

Flowers

An interconnected world

Over millions of years animals and plants have evolved to fill different roles in the rain forest. Each living thing relies on the presence of others in order to survive. This interconnected world has a delicate balance. If one species of plant or animal is threatened, it can affect the survival of many others.

Pollination

Very little wind enters through the top of the canopy, so trees and other plants need other ways of having their flowers pollinated. Many rely on insects and birds, such as the hummingbird, to carry away pollen, which sticks to their bodies as they feed on nectar. Bats pollinate flowers at night. The flowers of some trees grow on the trunks, far away from the leaves, making it easier for bats to find them.

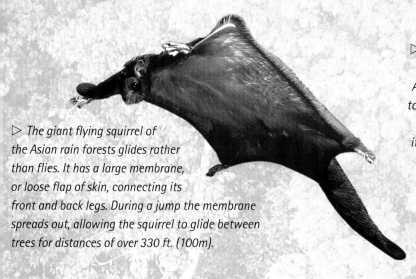

▷ The giant flying squirrel of the Asian rain forests glides rather than flies. It has a large membrane, or loose flap of skin, connecting its front and back legs. During a jump the membrane spreads out, allowing the squirrel to glide between trees for distances of over 330 ft. (100m).

▷ The slow-moving two-toed sloth of South and Central America relies on camouflage to avoid predators, such as the jaguar. Green algae grows in its fur, helping the sloth blend into the leafy canopy.

▽ Like many hummingbirds, the rufous-breasted hermit hummingbird uses cobwebs to build a tiny nest in the shelter of a leaf.

Moving through the canopy

For animals that cannot fly, moving around the canopy calls for great skill. Sloths and tree anteaters have sharp, powerful claws that they use to ease their way up to and through the canopy. The flying fox and some species of flying squirrels glide between trees. Monkeys are the most agile of the larger canopy dwellers. With their grasping hands and feet, they grip branches as they leap between trees. Monkeys of North and South America also have a prehensile tail—this means the tail can grip, working like a fifth hand.

Rain forest birds

Rain forests are home to over half of the world's bird species. Many birds are equipped with short, stubby wings to help them dart between the trunks and branches. Different-shaped beaks are specifically adapted for various feeding habits. For example, the long, hollow, and lightweight beak of the toucan is ideal for reaching hanging fruits, while the strong, hooked bills of parrots and macaws are designed to crack open nut and seed casings.

Predators in the canopy

The animals in the canopy are vulnerable to attack from all directions. Predatory birds, such as the powerful South American harpy eagle, swoop down from above to grab monkeys and sloths. Insects and small animals are potential prey for birds, so many are camouflaged to blend into the leafy background. The most common predators are the different species of snakes, many of which are highly poisonous. From below cats such as the margay and ocelot make occasional attacks. The cats live on the forest floor but climb up into the lower canopy at night to hunt.

▽ At 14 in. (35cm) long, the eyelash viper is one of the smallest poisonous snakes in the Central American rain forest. It feeds on frogs, lizards, small mammals, and birds.

Boreal forests

Boreal, or taiga, forests stretch through North America, Europe, and Asia, covering around 11 percent of earth's land surface. During the long and intensely cold winters, much of the groundwater in rivers, lakes, and ponds is frozen. The summers are short, and there may only be between 50 and 100 frost-free days in a year. Many birds and some land animals migrate from these forests during the winter, while others manage to live there all year round, coping in different ways with the extreme cold and the relative lack of food.

△ The capercaillie eats buds, shoots, berries, and seeds in the summer. In the winter it eats conifer shoots. Its chicks are often eaten by foxes, pine martens, and sparrow hawks.

▽ The wolverine is a hunter with powerful jaws and teeth. Its varied diet ranges from wasp larvae and eggs to lemmings, hares, and squirrels.

Coniferous forests

Forests of evergreen conifer trees dominate the vegetation of boreal forests and provide homes as well as food for many animals. The conifers are cone-shaped, so they can easily shed snow before their branches break under the weight. Their narrow, tough leaves can withstand strong winds and long periods of subzero temperatures. The waxy pine needles of many conifers protect the trees from the extreme cold, but they are very slow to decay once they have fallen to the ground. Coniferous forests rely on fungi to slowly break down the needles and release nutrients back into the soil.

△ Moose are the world's largest deer, with adult males weighing over half a ton. Moose eat twigs and bark in the winter and wade into thawed-out rivers and lakes in the summer to eat water plants.

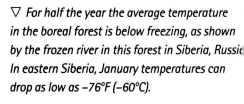

▽ For half the year the average temperature in the boreal forest is below freezing, as shown by the frozen river in this forest in Siberia, Russia. In eastern Siberia, January temperatures can drop as low as −76°F (−60°C).

△ *Beavers work together in well-organized family groups to fell trees and build dams and lodges. These provide shelter from the cold winters and a place to give birth to young.*

Protection from the cold

Animal life in boreal forests is limited by the severe winter. Some mammals hibernate, or sleep deeply, through the coldest months, while many bird species, such as the wood warbler, migrate south to a less harsh climate. Those animals that don't hibernate are usually covered with a thick insulating layer of fur or feathers. Many species are larger than their relatives in warmer climates, because their larger size helps them conserve body heat. Boreal forests are home to the world's largest deer (the moose) and weasel (the wolverine). The male capercaillie bird weighs up to 9 lbs (4kg), making it the largest member of the grouse family.

▽ *Some animals have evolved specific adaptations to help them reach cone seeds and use them as food. The crossbill's twisted beak allows it to crack into closed cones to get to the seeds before the cones open and the seeds are dispersed.*

▷ *A giant wood wasp drills a hole deep into the bark of a tree before laying its eggs in the hole. When the larvae emerge from their eggs, they spend two to three years maturing under the bark while feeding on the wood of the tree.*

Searching for food

Insect-feeding animals and birds usually migrate away from boreal forests in the winter. They return when warmer temperatures melt the groundwater, causing millions of insects to breed. Birds that eat cones and seeds, such as red crossbills and pine siskins, stay in boreal forests all year round. Some, such as the nutcracker (a member of the crow family) hide pinecone seeds in many different locations for the winter. Predators, such as the lynx and members of the weasel family (including wolverines, minks, and ermine), hunt snowshoe rabbits, voles, red squirrels, and other herbivores.

Temperate forests

Temperate forests and woodlands are found away from the heat of the equator and the extreme cold of the polar regions. They lie mainly above the Tropic of Cancer and below the Tropic of Capricorn, in regions with a great variation between summer and winter climates. Much of Europe and North America were covered by temperate forests until trees were cleared to make room for farmland, houses, and industries. At one time 80 percent of Great Britain was covered by trees. That figure is now only ten percent.

△ *Some animals, such as this hazel dormouse, survive the winter by using up their reserves of fat during hibernation. To use less energy, the animal's body temperature and heart rate drops.*

◁ *A forest of deciduous aspen trees show their spectacular fall colors in the Rocky Mountains, Colorado. Aspens provide valuable food for elk and deer herds.*

Surviving the winter

In temperate forests the short days of winter provide too little sunlight for trees to really photosynthesize, while their roots struggle to absorb water from the cold, often frozen, ground. So trees rest during the winter and protect themselves in different ways. Coniferous trees, such as pines and firs, have needle-shaped leaves with a waxy coating. This keeps moisture within the tree. Conifers also have built-in antifreeze to protect them from the frost. This means they can keep their leaves through the winter and start to photosynthesize as soon as spring arrives.

Deciduous trees

Most broad-leaved trees are deciduous. This means they shed their leaves in the winter to prevent damage from the cold and to stop water from evaporating from the leaves that their roots could not easily replace because the ground is frozen. In the fall the trees take back nutrients from their leaves, which change color from green to yellow and red. Then the leaves fall. The fallen leaves are broken down by decomposers, like fungi and earthworms, to create a rich humus. The humus begins to decay and release nutrients into the soil in time for spring, when the growing season begins.

▽ *This rotting tree log is home to a range of fungi and green mosses. As it decomposes a rotting log can provide a home or breeding ground for toads and salamanders, as well as worms and millipedes, which attract moles, shrews and other insect-hunting animals. Eventually the log will fall apart and decay into humus, enriching the soil.*

▷ The monarch butterfly is found mainly in North and Central America. Monarchs absorb poison from their diet of milkweed plants, and their bright colors are a warning to predators that they are dangerous to eat.

◁ Insects are a valuable food source for many bird species in deciduous temperate forests. Here a garden warbler feeds a caterpillar to its chicks.

▽ Monkey puzzle trees in Conquillio National Park, Chile. This tree is an evergreen tree with stiff, overlapping leaves, growing to a height of 150 ft. (45m). Its seeds are an important food source for people and some animals.

Woodland wildlife

Temperate woodlands provide rich sources of food in the spring, summer, and fall. Most of the food that comes from trees in the form of leaves, nuts, flowers, and fruits is high up in the branches. This attracts birds and squirrels. Trees also provide a home and food source for a vast number of insects. A single mature oak tree, for example, can support over 35,000 caterpillars eating its leaves at one time. Other insects eat bark or bore and chew their way into a tree's trunk. The millions of insects in a temperate forest are a vital part of the food web. They are eaten by predatory insects, such as ladybugs and other beetles, as well as many species of insect-eating birds.

The forest floor

In the spring the forest floor is carpeted by flowering plants, such as the snowdrop, crocus, and primrose. They grow in the sunlight that streams through the bare trees above them. In the summer plants adapted to life in the shade—ferns and mosses—thrive in the damp and relatively dark conditions on the forest floor. These plants and the insects they attract are food for small mammals, such as mice, voles, and chipmunks. Predators that feed on these animals include foxes and some owls and weasels. In many temperate forests deer graze on the leaves of shrubs and bushes.

◁ Bluebells flower from early April to June, making full use of the sunlight before the deciduous trees above them are fully covered with adult leaves.

33

People and forests

Forests, especially tropical rain forests, are home to many tribes of people and provide the world with many important products, from food to timber. As well as balancing the levels of carbon dioxide in the atmosphere, they provide habitats for hundreds of thousands of plant and animal species that might perish elsewhere. Yet forests are constantly under threat because of a range of human activities—from harvesting trees for timber, pulp, and paper to clearing away forests for the land they stand on.

△ Many roads are carved through forests to improve transportation links. This road runs through the largely unspoiled boreal forests of Kuusamo in Finland.

Rain forest tribes

Over 1,000 tribes of forest people live in the rain forests. They obtain all they need from the forest and often live in small groups, yet they need a large area of forest to support them. The Pygmies are Central African forest dwellers. Their small size allows them to move easily through the thick tree growth as they hunt monkeys and gather honey and fruit.

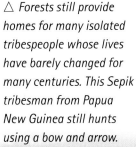

△ Forests still provide homes for many isolated tribespeople whose lives have barely changed for many centuries. This Sepik tribesman from Papua New Guinea still hunts using a bow and arrow.

The Yamomami live in the Amazon rain forest. As well as hunting animals, they cultivate gardens in the forest, growing plants for medicine, food, and building materials. The Yamomami were only discovered by outsiders in the 1950s, yet already their numbers have dropped. Their habitat is being destroyed by foresters, while tribespeople are killed by outside diseases, such as measles and influenza, against which they have no natural defense.

▽ In Chile almost a million acres of native forest have been cut down and replaced by plantations of fast-growing imported trees, such as Monterey pine and the eucalyptus (below). Native animals have trouble surviving in these single-species, or monoculture, plantations.

Forest destruction

Forests have long been ravaged for their timber and to convert the land they stand on into farming fields, mining territories, or new settlements. Many of the large temperate forests in the U.S., Europe, and New Zealand have disappeared as the human population has grown. Large areas of boreal forests and rain forests are under threat from modern timber collecting techniques that reach into the most isolated areas. The forests of southern Canada are being harmed by acid rain from industries in the northern United States, while Scandinavian forests are suffering the same fate from pollution generated in western Europe. Fires, occurring naturally in a dry summer or caused by thoughtless human visitors, can also destroy large tracts of forest.

◁ *These trees in northern Europe have been damaged by acid rain. This is created when industrial pollution and motor vehicle emissions mix with oxygen and water vapor in the air.*

Forest products

Wood has been the main forest product for thousands of years. Different timbers are used for different jobs. Elm, resistant to rotting in water, is used for harbor piers and lock gates. Mahogany and rosewood have beautiful, rich colors and are used for decorative furniture. Many plants, such as coffee, rubber, avocado, and the kola nuts used in soft drinks, all originated in rain forests.

◁ *Rain forest plants and trees are used in 20 percent of the world's medicines. This Madagascar periwinkle contains a large number of useful substances, including vincristine and vinblastine. These are used to manufacture medecines that fight cancer.*

▽ *Christmas Island, 225 mi. (360km) south of Java, is home to a number of rare bird species. Phosphate mining has devastated parts of the forest, but now most of the island has been designated as a national park, and trees are being replanted.*

Saving forests

There are many ways in which the impact of deforestation—the destruction of forests—can be reduced, from recycling paper to protecting endangered forest species. Preserving the remaining forest areas and planting new trees to replace those already lost are the priorities. Many countries have turned large forests into protected national parks, while hundreds of programs are returning trees to urban wastelands and areas affected by drought or the spread of deserts. The Green Belt Movement in Kenya, for example, has planted over ten million trees in 20 years. Poorer countries often rely on their forests to generate money for their people. Sustainable forestry—planting new trees to replace those cut down—is one way to protect this source of income.

African grasslands

The tropical grasslands, or savannas, of Africa support bushes, scattered trees, and an abundance of grasses. They are hot all year round, but they have long dry seasons and shorter wet seasons. The grasslands are a food-rich environment for insects, some birds, and large herds of plant-eating creatures, such as wildebeest, zebras, gazelles, and giraffes. Different animals feed on different plants, enabling the grasslands to support a large number of grazers that in return are an ample food source for predators, including big cats, crocodiles, and birds of prey.

△ The black-headed weaverbird builds a nest from grass and twigs, hanging it high in a tree.

▽ A giraffe's extremely long neck allows it to reach the high branches of acacia trees.

Safety from predators

The wide-open grasslands of Africa provide no hiding places from predators. Grazing animals have developed three main methods of defense. Some, such as the elephant and hippopotamus, have evolved to be a large size and to have thick skin, making them hard to attack and wound. Animals such as the zebra and wildebeest live in large herds. Herds provide greater protection for the young—more sets of eyes to keep on the lookout for danger, and the sheer mass of bodies can confuse a predator. Many herd animals use speed to escape attacks. They have long legs and hooves instead of toes, allowing them to run for long periods at top speed.

△ As well as wild herds, the African grasslands support some domesticated animals. The Masai people of Kenya rely on herds of cattle, goats, and sheep for food. Sometimes cattle blood is a major food source for the Masai.

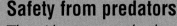

▷ Migrating herds of zebras and wildebeest drink at the Mara River in Kenya.

Megafauna

African grasslands are home to the largest land animals on earth—hippos, rhinoceroses, and the largest of them all, the African elephant. An adult male elephant stands 13 ft. (4m) tall and can weigh seven tons. It uses its flexible trunk to feed roots, grass, and trees to its mouth. White rhinos are grass eaters, weighing up to three tons. Living in small groups, they mark out their territory with piles of dung and urine. With their immense size and power and a thick protective layer of skin, megafauna have few predators and do not need to move fast. Their most serious threat comes from humans. Elephants are killed for their ivory tusks, and rhinoceros horns are prized as a medicine in Asia. Populations of both animals have been slashed, with only 5,000 white rhinos left in the wild in the year 2000.

▷ *African elephant numbers have been greatly reduced by ivory poachers. Tusks collected from poachers are burned* (left).

▽ *Elephants live in close-knit family groups, which protect sick and young members. When a lion—the only predator of an elephant calf—threatens, the elephants form a circle around the calf to warn off the attacker.*

Great migrations

Living in giant herds provides some safety from predators, but it also poses problems for grazers. With herd sizes in the tens of thousands, land cannot support such grazing for long, and the herds have to travel to different places to fine food. In the Serengeti grasslands, wildebeest herds start an annual migration in May as the dry season arrives and food runs out. They head north to the long grasses of Lake Victoria and then move again to fresh grazing lands across the Mara River. By November they return to their starting point, where new grass will support them until they begin another migration the following year.

African predators

The grazing animals of Africa's grasslands are under risk of attack from a range of powerful hunters. On land the big cats are the most well-known predators; crocodiles lurk in water holes, lakes, and rivers; and birds of prey are a threat from the air. These animals all have strong claws or jaws to grab and bring down their prey and sharp teeth to slice through hides and flesh—but catching prey calls for raw speed, teamwork, or great intelligence.

Overlapping roles

The predators of the African grasslands would struggle if they all hunted the same creatures and ate in the same way. So lions and crocodiles attack larger grazing animals, while cheetahs and leopards target smaller ones, such as Thomson's gazelle. Rodents, insects, small birds, and amphibians are hunted by the zorilla (a relative of the skunk), wild dogs, and birds of prey, such as the eagle and secretary bird. Once a kill is made a series of creatures benefit. The predator takes its share, but other animals move in to feed as well. Scavengers, such as jackals, hyenas, and vultures, feed on carrion—the dead, rotting remains of other animal's kills. In their role as decomposers scavengers play a vital part in the grasslands ecosystem.

Cheetahs

Leopards

Lions

Hyenas

Wildebeest

Antelope

Baboons

Giraffes

Zebras

Acacia

Grasses

△ Lions, the top savanna predators, are not hunted by other animals, but they are threatened by drought, habitat destruction, a lack of food, and killing by humans.

▽ The Nile crocodile waits for animals, such as this wildebeest, to come for a drink and then drags its prey underwater to drown it.

△ A lioness forces down a waterbuck in Kruger National Park, South Africa.

Cheetahs

Smaller and lighter than other big cats, cheetahs are built for speed. They sit on rocky outcrops called kopjes, on the lookout for young wildebeest and smaller gazelles. Cheetahs hunt alone or sometimes in groups of two or three, keeping low in the grass to get as close as possible without alerting their prey. Their phenomenal burst of speed can be kept up only over short distances. Cheetahs eat quickly after a kill because they are small enough to be driven away from their prey by scavengers, such as vultures and hyenas.

▷ A cheetah has long legs, a streamlined head, wide nostrils to take in plenty of oxygen, and unlike all other big cats, claws that don't retract. These features, plus a highly flexible spine, allow cheetahs to reach speeds of over 68 mph (110km/h), making it the world's fastest land animal.

Hyenas

Hyenas look clumsy, with their oversized heads and short back legs, but they can reach speeds of 40 mph (65km/h). They spend most of the day in underground dens and then hunt their own prey and scavenge the kills of other animals at night. Hyenas hunt in large packs that harass herds of zebras or wildebeest until one is separated and brought down by the sheer weight of numbers. A hyena's jaws are so powerful that they can shear through a zebra's thigh bone. After a kill individuals tear off a chunk of meat and eat it away from the others.

△ Hyenas are successful hunters and scavengers, capable of defending food from other animals. This spotted hyena is chasing away a vulture.

▽ Lions live in family groups called prides, which include several females and up to four males. Although the male lions don't take part in the hunt, they are the first to eat. They are followed by the adult females and then the cubs. In tough times the cubs are the first to starve.

Lions

Lions are the largest of the African big cats, but they are slower than some of their prey, reaching top speeds of 36 mph (58km/h). Only female lions hunt, both in the day and at night, relying on teamwork to ambush their prey. Up to ten lionesses approach a herd, single out an individual, and spread out. One or two of the team charge the prey, forcing it toward the other lionesses hiding in the grass. The prey is usually killed by suffocation—a lioness clamps her mouth over the animal's mouth and nostrils or bites its windpipe.

Temperate grasslands

Grasslands develop in areas that are too dry for forests to form and too wet to be deserts. Temperate grasslands have warm summers and cold winters, yet overall they tend to be cooler than savanna grasslands. Temperate grasslands include the veld in South Africa, the pampas of South America, and the central Asia steppes. Grasslands once covered one quarter of the planet's land, but most of this is now used for agriculture. Grasslands still cover wide areas, but they can be extremely delicate and easily disrupted, as has happened in North America.

△ The buffalo is the largest animal on the plains of North America. Adults weigh up to 1,430 lbs (650kg).

▽ Burrowing owls use old prairie dog burrows as an underground nest for their chicks. They line the burrow with animal dung. The dung generates heat as it decomposes, helps mask the scent of the owls from predators, and also attracts dung beetles—a source of food for the chicks.

Buffalo and the plains

The North American plains and prairies once occupied 1 million sq. mi. (2.5 million sq km) and were home to over 50 million buffalo. This large grazing mammal mainly eats tough grasses that are relatively low in nutrients. Buffalo were the main food source for native Americans, who hunted them selectively and used every piece of their prey for tools, food, clothing, and shelter. With the arrival of European settlers, an ecosystem that had lasted thousands of years was severely disrupted. The settlers used horses and guns to hunt large numbers of buffalo. In the early 1870s, 2.5 million buffalo were killed each year. By 1880 only a few hundred were left. A conservation program saved the buffalo from extinction, and herd numbers are now around 200,000 across North America.

A changing ecosystem

The loss of buffalo herds was just one of the many changes to the grasslands ecosystem. Farmers began to heavily exploit the rich, fertile soil of many grassland areas. They grew wheat and other grains, removing the habitat that local plants and animals needed to survive. The wheat was not as hardy as the native grass it replaced, nor did its roots bind the soil in place as well.

△ The prairie rattlesnake needs an underground refuge for the winter months. Snakes cannot dig their own holes, so they find a rock crevice or use the burrows of prairie dogs as a winter home.

Dust bowl

A period of drought in the 1930s left the soil of the North American grasslands to be exposed and then blown away by strong winds, creating a giant "dust bowl." Today the plains and prairies are used to grow crops because of modern farming and irrigation techniques. Three quarters of the United States' wheat exports now come from this area, but many species of wild plants and animals have suffered as a result.

▽ Prairie dogs live in an enormous network of burrows in family groups called cotteries. They mark the entrance to each burrow with mounds of soil and post lookouts to keep watch for predators, such as eagles and coyotes.

Prairie dogs

The lack of trees on the plains means that many animals need to look elsewhere for a home. Without a deep network of tree roots, the ground is ideal for burrowing animals such as prairie dogs, a species of ground squirrel. They dig enormous systems of burrows with separate bathrooms, bedrooms, and birth chambers. Each system can extend for miles. Old burrows are used as homes by other animals, such as owls, black-legged ferrets, and swift foxes. At one time it was estimated that over 800 million prairie dogs existed in North America. Numbers are now closer to two million after a poisoning campaign by farmers in the early 1900s and turning 98 percent of their habitat into farmland.

▽ Yellowstone National Park is home to around 3,500 buffalo. Although they look big and slow, adult buffalo can gallop at speeds of up to 28 mph (45km/h).

● People and grasslands

Grasslands are highly productive ecosystems, providing habitats and food for a wide range of plant and wild animal species. They also support large human populations all over the world with the products they provide. A balanced grassland region recycles its water and keeps its fertile soil in place, allowing many different organisms to live there. Grasslands are also a major source of carbon—over one third of earth's carbon is found in grasslands, mainly in the soil. Unfortunately the activities of humans have had a devastating effect on some grassland areas.

△ Unspoiled grassland areas are home to large numbers of wild flowering plants. The California poppy is native to grasslands that stretch along western North America, from British Columbia to southern California. Native Americans in some parts of California used to boil and eat the poppy's leaves and stems.

◁ The state of Montana contains around four million acres (2 million ha) of wheat fields, which produced 2.62 million tons of wheat in 2001. Only North Dakota and Kansas produce more wheat.

Threats to grasslands

Grasslands face a number of threats, including overgrazing and desertification—the spread of desert areas. The most common threat is when they are deliberately converted by humans for other uses, such as for new urban areas and in particular for agriculture. Converting huge areas to grow crops removes the natural habitat of many living things. New roads divide and fragment any remaining habitats that can also be disrupted by the introduction by humans of nonnative species. Wild animals and plants are suddenly seen as pests and are wiped out by hunting and the use of pesticides, herbicides, and poisons. As farming is conducted on an ever larger scale the diversity of life in a region tends to fall.

▽ Most of the North American prairies were plowed to produce farmland for growing grains, such as wheat and corn. In the 1930s poor farmland management, a long drought, and strong winds eroded much of the fertile soil, creating a dust bowl.

The pampas

Argentina and part of Uruguay are home to wide, mainly flat, grassy plains called the pampas. Covering approximately 294,000 sq. mi. (760,000 sq km), the pampas have undergone many changes since the introduction of cattle by Spanish colonial rulers. By the 1800s large cattle herds roamed much of the pampas. Today huge cattle ranches called *estancias* are run by cowhands known as *gauchos*. Much of the remaining pampas grassland has been converted to growing crops such as wheat, corn, soybeans, and fruits. Apart from losing their natural homes and feeding grounds, many wild animals, such as rheas, the pampas deer, and several species of wildcats, have been hunted for their skins or killed because they are pests.

△ Geoffroy's cat is found in isolated forests and grasslands in Bolivia, Paraguay, Uruguay, and southern Argentina. Until the late 1980s it was heavily hunted for its fur, with 25 cat pelts needed to make one single fur coat.

▷ The skilled cattle herders of the pampas are known as gauchos. They immobilize and catch cattle using a boleadora, three stones tied together with a rope that wraps itself around the legs of a cow when thrown accurately.

Mongolian steppes

The large central Asian country of Mongolia is one of the most sparsely populated countries in the world. Yet because it is poor, has little industry, and much of its land is barren desert, the pressures on its grasslands, known as the Mongolian steppes, are severe. Livestock products such as meat, milk, and hides make up one third of its economy, and with a population that is rising by two percent every year, the pressures on Mongolia's fertile land to feed everyone are growing. As a result, overgrazing is widespread. In addition around 23 percent of Mongolia's land is at risk of desertification. This forces wildlife into overcompetition for remaining food and habitat space.

▽ Mongolian herders move their livestock to summer grazing ground near Lake Hovsgol in northwestern Mongolia. Mongolian nomads sometimes have to contend with harsh conditions. In 2001 an extremely dry summer followed by a severe winter caused the loss of more than three million livestock.

4 Deserts

With less than 10 in. (250mm) of rainfall every year, deserts are the driest places on the planet and occupy over 20 percent of the land surface. Of all the world's environments deserts offer the greatest challenge to life. The soil is so poor that very few plants can grow, and there is little shelter from the strong winds that blow soil and sand across the surface. In some deserts temperatures can fluctuate from extremely hot (over 100°F/40°C) in the day to below freezing at night. Deserts are often inhabited by unusual plants and animals that have adapted to the tough conditions.

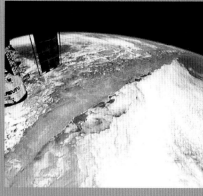

△ Seen from space, the Atacama Desert of Chile is a cloudless strip, running for 590 mi. (950km) between the Pacific Ocean and the Andes Mountains. In some parts of the desert rain may not fall for a year or more.

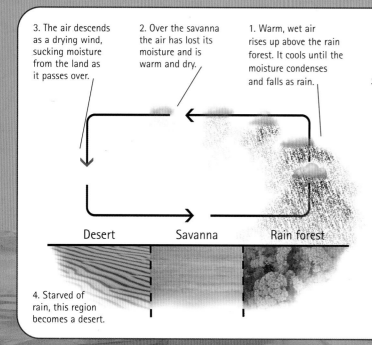

3. The air descends as a drying wind, sucking moisture from the land as it passes over.

2. Over the savanna the air has lost its moisture and is warm and dry.

1. Warm, wet air rises up above the rain forest. It cools until the moisture condenses and falls as rain.

Desert   Savanna   Rain forest

4. Starved of rain, this region becomes a desert.

◁ Tropical deserts exist approximately 930 mi. (1,500km) either side of the equator—in the Tropic of Cancer to the north and in the Tropic of Capricorn to the south. The Sahara Desert of North Africa, the Thar Desert of the Indian subcontinent, and the Victoria Desert of Australia are all tropical deserts.

Continental deserts

Different types of desert are created in different ways. Continental deserts, such as the Gobi in Mongolia and China, form because they are so far from the sea that little rain ever reaches them.

Coastal deserts and rain shadow deserts

Coastal deserts form near cold seas. Air passing over the sea is cooled down, creating clouds that drop their moisture over the sea as rain or mist before reaching the land. Africa's Namib Desert is an example of a coastal desert. A rain shadow desert occurs where a mountain range lies in the path of winds carrying rain from the sea. The winds cool down over the mountains and release almost all of the water they carry as rain. The land on the other side of the mountains receives hardly any rainfall and becomes a desert. The Rocky Mountains in North America and the Great Dividing Range in Australia have created deserts this way.

△ The shovel-snouted lizard lives in the Namib Desert, which stretches for 1,240 mi. (2,000km) along the west coast of southern Africa. When the temperature soars into the high nineties, the lizard uses its wide snout to burrow beneath the sand.

Desert surfaces

People think of deserts as sandy wildernesses, but not all deserts are covered in sand. Desert winds can blow sand and other light materials away, exposing the heavier gravel, rocks, and stones below. The sand is often deposited in one area as a great sea of sand dunes. These seas are called ergs, and individual dunes can be hundreds of feet high. Sometimes a strong, turbulent wind scoops up the surface sand, generating a sandstorm that may travel hundreds of miles.

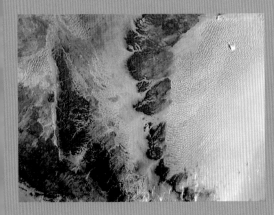

◁ *Areas of sand, stony ground, and rocky outcrops can all be found in the same desert. This picture from space shows part of the Sahara Desert. The sandy area is a vast expanse of sand dunes, called the Murzuk Sand Sea, in the North African country of Libya. Both the sand dunes and the rocky outcrops support almost no life.*

△ *The surface of this desert on the Colorado plateau is made of sandstone—the remains of desert sand dunes that have hardened into rock over millions of years.*

Water in the desert

Rainfall is not the only source of water in a desert. Coastal deserts receive moisture from mists that roll in off of the sea. Mists occur regularly in the Namib Desert in Africa and in the deserts in Peru and California. Oases are another source of water. Deep underground, layers of rock trap water and stop it from draining away. Where these rock layers reach the surface and are eroded to form a hollow, the water is exposed. Life tends to spring up around the water, forming an oasis.

▽ *An oasis is an area of fertile land in a desert supplied all year round with fresh water. Some oases form naturally around underground springs, others are created by humans. They are often the only source of surface water for hundreds of miles.*

Deserts
🌵 Water of life

Deserts are defined by their lack of water. There can be years between rainfalls, and the key to survival is making the most of the tiny amount of existing water. Desert plants are the masters here—by gathering and storing water they then make it available to animals higher up the food chain. Because of the water contained in the plants, many desert animals never drink at all—the herbivores eat the plants, and the carnivores eat the herbivores. However, for those animals that must drink, some unique solutions are required for survival.

△ In times of drought African quiver trees can shed some of their branches to reduce water loss and ensure their survival.

Gathering and keeping water

Desert plants suck up water from a wide area, using far-reaching webs of fine roots. Many plants store the water in a large underground taproot, out of reach of the sun's soaring temperatures. Others store it in their stems, which are often covered in a waxy, waterproof coat to reduce water loss from evaporation. Because of their large surface area, leaves lose a lot of water through evaporation, so in desert plants they are often small or nonexistent. During droughts some plants can actually shed their leaves—or even whole branches— to minimize their water loss.

▽ The welwitschia plant of the Namib Desert has two 23-foot (7-m)- long leaves that collect fog droplets and funnel them to a buried taproot in the center of the plant.

△ Cactuses have special concertina-shaped stems that can swell with water without splitting. To minimize water loss from evaporation, they have spines instead of leaves and photosynthesize through their stems. The spines also prevent attack by thirsty animals.

Animals and water

For those animals that need to drink, the desert poses huge challenges. They must be able to travel long distances between water sources and store water efficiently in the meantime. Camels can hold up to 10 gallons (40*l*) of water in the fat of their humps, allowing them to travel up to 620 mi. (1,000km) without drinking. In contrast, the sandgrouse must drink every day, but while adults can fly far to find water, their flightless chicks cannot. The adults solve this problem by sitting in water holes, soaking up water into their spongelike feathers, and then carrying it to the chicks. Another ingenious adaptation is that of the fogstand beetle, which collects water from mist by allowing it to condense on its body.

▷ *When sea mist rolls in across the Namib Desert, the fogstand beetle rushes to the tops of sand dunes, lifts its back into the air, and waits for fog to condense on its shell. The water droplets then run down its raised back and into its mouth.*

△ *The sandgrouse's feathers are specifically adapted to retain water. They must absorb a large amount because much of it will be lost on the flight back to their nest.*

▽ *The spadefoot toad emerges from the ground after the rains to mate and lay eggs. The eggs hatch, and the young frogs retreat underground before drought returns.*

▽ *For a brief period after the annual rains the desert is full of life. Plants and animals take advantage of the season to reproduce and store food and water.*

The coming of the rains

If rain eventually comes, the desert bursts into life. Amphibians emerge from hibernation to breed in the temporary desert pools. Meanwhile seeds that have laid dormant, or inactive, can now begin to grow—but only if there is sufficient water. Many seeds are covered in a chemical that stops them from growing unless it is completely washed off, which only a lot of rain will do. The seeds grow quickly, flowering within days to attract the insects that follow the rains. After pollination the plants set seed, wither, and die, having lived only a few weeks.

4 Surviving the heat

If animals become too hot, they die. Overheating is a major threat to survival in the extreme temperatures of some deserts. Animals in other biomes cool down by sweating or panting. Water evaporates from their bodies, taking away heat as it leaves. But in the desert where every drop of water is vital, animals stay cool in other ways. Many desert animals are pale in color because pale shades reflect more heat than darker colors. Other ways to avoid the heat are burrowing underground, seeking shelter in the shade, and foraging for food at night.

△ Scorpions are mainly found in desert areas, although some live in other habitats. Female scorpions give birth to many young that spend the first week or two of their lives on their mothers' back. Once they climb down they lead independent lives.

△ A gemsbok oryx in the Kalahari Desert, South Africa. Oryx spend the day seeking shade. They never drink and rely on obtaining water from the plants they eat at night.

The cool night

Most desert animals are active at night when the desert is much cooler. Spiders and scorpions scurry out of their lairs to hunt. Scorpions use hairs that are highly sensitive to air movements to track down insects, small rodents, and lizards. Scorpions grip their prey with powerful pincers, and then rip it apart with strong jaws. A scorpion only uses its stinger on large prey. Night is also the best time for plant-eating creatures to eat. Dew forms on the plants, increasing their water content from a few percent to as much as 40 percent.

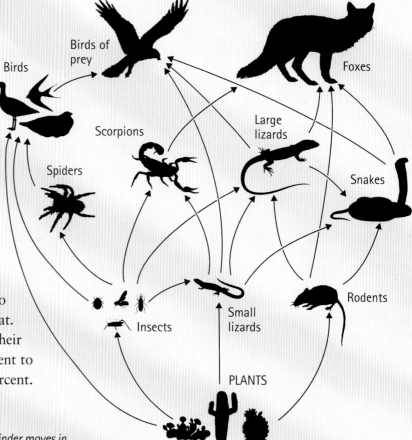

Birds of prey

Birds

Foxes

Scorpions

Large lizards

Spiders

Snakes

Insects

Small lizards

Rodents

PLANTS

◁ The sidewinder moves in S-shaped waves. This means that only a tiny part of the snake's body touches the burning-hot ground.

△ The food web in the desert is smaller and less complex than in other biomes. Foxes, birds of prey, and snakes are at the top of the food chains.

Going underground

The surface of the desert can reach temperatures over 160°F (70°C), yet just a few inches below ground it is much cooler. Many animals live underground to avoid the potentially lethal heat on the surface. The sandfish is a lizard with small, close-fitting scales that allow it to wriggle through the sand with a side-to-side movement similar to a fish. Some desert animals, such as desert toads, remain dormant deep underground until the summer rains fill ponds. Then they climb to the surface, breed, lay eggs, and replenish their body supplies of food and water before returning underground.

△ A Grant's desert golden mole catches a locust in the Namib Desert. Golden moles live mainly underground, burrowing through the sand with their short, strong forearms. Because they are blind and deaf, golden moles use their excellent sense of smell to detect lizards, insects, and spiders.

Desert homes

For many desert animals home is a burrow dug into the sand that protects them from the sun. A fennec fox's burrow is a tunnel up to 33 ft. (10m) long, and the kangaroo rat's burrow contains storage space for food. Camel spiders and wind scorpions block their burrow entrances with plugs of sand to keep out the heat. The giant saguaro cactuses in the Sonoran Desert are home to several bird species. Ladderback woodpeckers chisel out holes in cactuses high above the ground, where it is cooler. When the woodpeckers move on, desert owls inhabit their old nesting holes.

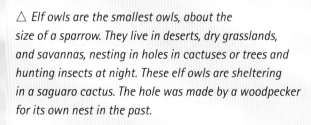

△ Elf owls are the smallest owls, about the size of a sparrow. They live in deserts, dry grasslands, and savannas, nesting in holes in cactuses or trees and hunting insects at night. These elf owls are sheltering in a saguaro cactus. The hole was made by a woodpecker for its own nest in the past.

▷ The fennec fox lives in deserts in northern Africa and the Middle East. It is the smallest fox but has large ears that act as cooling devices. The fennec spends most of the day in an underground burrow. It hunts at night, using its large ears to detect insects and rodents.

🜨 People and deserts

Just as animals have found ways to survive in
the world's deserts, so have people. Some people
live near oases, farming and living off of fertile land
close to water supplies. Other desert people live as
nomads, moving from place to place with herds
of animals or carving out an existence by hunting,
gathering, and trading. The harsh environment has
a great impact on how desert people live, but the
human impact on deserts is even more dramatic.
Many deserts are growing larger as neighboring
areas are overfarmed and poorly managed.

▽ A Mongolian nomad and his tent home, known as
a yurt. Traditional yurts have a wooden frame covered
with felt or animal skin. The yurt is pitched
wherever the nomad finds good
pasture for his herds.

△ Bedouin people live a nomadic existence
in the Sahara, Syrian, and Arabian deserts. They
herd their animals across the desert, following
the rains in search of grazing land. Flowing robes
and headdresses shield the Bedouin from the
fierce sun and wind-driven sands.

Desert nomads

In the past most desert dwellers were nomads
who herded goats, camels, and cattle, or they were
hunter-gatherers such as the San people of the Kalahari
Desert. Others, like the Tuareg, controlled the trade
routes of the Sahara Desert. They carried gold and ivory
in large caravans of camels. Today life is very different.
Droughts have reduced the size of the nomads' herds,
and national borders make it impossible to wander as
freely as in the past. New roads have cut back on the
importance of camel caravans, which now mainly carry
salt rather than the riches of before. Many desert people
have been forced to settle and seek work in oases
or in towns away from the desert.

◁ For thousands of years people have used camels
to travel across desert regions. These Bactrian camels
can carry a heavy load on average 30 mi. (50km) per day.
All camels store food as fat in their humps and can go
without water for more than two weeks.

Desertification

Desertification is the spread of desert environments. It is a growing problem in many parts of the world—as much as 23,000 sq. mi. (60,000 sq km) of new deserts are created every year. These lands are less able to support any life—wild animals, livestock, crops, and people. Desertification is caused by the planet becoming warmer and drier, which means there is less water to support plants and animals. Human activity also has a major effect. Deforestation, overgrazing, and certain types of farming result in the ground losing its plant covering. The exposed topsoil, which is vital to plant growth, may be blown away. Without topsoil water runs away, wells and springs dry up, and what plant life remains is threatened.

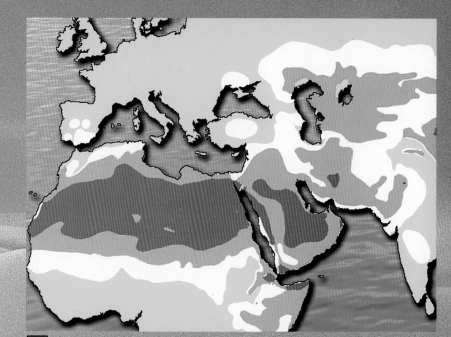

■ Extreme desert
□ Arid zone at risk of further desertification
□ Semiarid zone at risk of desertification

△ This map shows the spread of deserts in northern Africa and Eurasia.

Desert management

Stopping a desert from spreading is difficult and costly. Animals and people are moved from land under threat to avoid overgrazing and to allow plants to recover or be replanted. Keeping the soil in place is vital. Shelters from the wind, known as windbreaks, reduce the amount of soil blown away. Covering the soil with a layer of leaves, straw, and sawdust is called mulching. This enriches the soil, keeps it in place, and cuts down water loss due to evaporation. Irrigation is the channeling of water to a dry area. One technique is called center-pivot irrigation. Water is pumped up to the surface from deep underground and distributed over a large circular area.

△ The Sahel is a dry savanna region south of the Sahara Desert. Severe droughts and an increase in the number of people and grazing animals have caused major desertification. In some places, the Sahara Desert has spread south more than 62 mi. (100km) since the 1950s.

▽ A rock painting from A.D. 300 shows a cow and herder in the Sahara region, suggesting that the Sahara once supported grazing animals.

▽ Seen from space, the desert near the Tuwayq Mountains in Saudi Arabia shows the effects of center-pivot irrigation. Dark circles are watered areas where crops are being grown. Lighter circles are fields currently without crops.

The tundra

In the far north where the trees end and the Arctic ice begins lies the tundra. This bleak, windswept biome makes up 15 percent of earth's land area. The soil under the surface is permanently frozen, and mosses, lichen, and a few shrubs are the only plants that can survive the long, snowbound winters. But during the brief summer, flowers bloom in the millions, and migrating creatures arrive to eat and breed before the winter sets in again.

△ The Arctic fox's pure white winter coat provides the perfect camouflage. It preys mainly on lemmings, storing some of its kill in ice caverns for when times are tough.

▽ In the short summer, which begins in June, the surface temperature can reach 77°F (25°C) and the tundra bursts into life. Plants such as these lupins carpet the landscape, while insects thrive in the warm conditions, attracting thousands of migrating birds.

Hardy survivors

During the dark winter, when temperatures can fall as low as –76°F (–60°C), the tundra is one of the most inhospitable places on earth. However, there are creatures that live here all year round. Lemmings survive the bitter cold in complex underground tunnels, feeding on the roots of plants above them. The lemmings then provide food for hunters, like the Arctic fox and snowy owl.

▷ Wolf packs appear from the boreal forests in the summer, following the herds of caribou (below). With some teamwork they pick off weak members of the herds and then chase them for hours until the weary beasts can be attacked safely. Flocks of ravens follow the wolves, stealing tidbits from their kill.

◁ *Lemmings are a key part of the tundra food chain. Remaining active in burrows under the winter snows, lemmings can produce eight litters of nine young each year. This huge population sustains many of the tundra's predators.*

Migration routes

Millions of migrating birds flock to the tundra to breed in the summer, attracted by the huge number of insects there to feed their young. The relatively few predators present make the tundra a particularly inviting place for birds such as the Arctic tern. These long-distance travelers fly 21,700 mi. (35,000km) each year, journeying from summertime in the Antarctic to summertime in the Arctic and back again. They navigate by the sun and stars and by a built-in compass that is sensitive to changes in the earth's magnetic field.

The land reborn

With the coming of summer, the snow melts, and the soil at the surface defrosts. The ground beneath is still frozen, however, and prevents the meltwater from draining away. This makes the tundra in the summer a swampy place, ideal for insect life, such as mosquitoes, blackflies, and springtails.

Safety in numbers

Every summer huge herds of caribou head north, leaving the forests in which they have spent the winter, to graze on the rich vegetation that blooms briefly across the tundra. The caribou move constantly, never overgrazing the delicate lichens, which can take up to 40 years to regrow. Wolves shadow them at all times—if they attack, the caribou form a circle around their calves. In the winter hunters and hunted return to the forests.

▽ *Snowy owls catch lemmings by using their highly-developed hearing to pinpoint tiny rustling sounds under the snow.*

△ *Large numbers of caribou return to the relative safety of the forests during the winter months. They migrate in herds of up to 10,000 animals.*

The Arctic ice

North of the boreal forests and the Arctic tundra lies the Arctic ice cap. This area of sea and ice is intensely cold. During the winter, which lasts almost six months, the sun does not rise in the Arctic skies, sending temperatures plummeting as low as −76°F (−60°C). This icy world supports almost no plant growth, but the waters around and beneath it are teeming with life. Mammals such as the polar bear, Arctic fox, walrus, and seal have adapted to the bitter cold, insulated by thick layers of fat called blubber.

Growing and shrinking

The North Pole is covered by an immense sheet of ice, most of which floats on the Arctic Ocean. This is a polar ice cap, forming an area larger than Europe. The boundaries of the sheet are constantly changing. In the spring the edges of the ice cap start to melt, causing large chunks of ice to break away from the main mass. By midsummer the polar ice cap has almost halved in size. The ice returns to its full size in the winter, but scientists have noted that overall the ice cap appears to be shrinking greatly—both in thickness and area. Many scientists believe that global warming is to blame.

△ The Arctic pack ice grows and shrinks with the seasons. This map shows its average size over a year.

▽ The orca, or killer whale, uses echolocation—a type of sonar—to detect prey. It emits high-pitched clicks and senses the sounds as they bounce back off of solid objects such as fish, sea turtles, seals, and even other whales.

▷ Ice breaking off from the edge of the Arctic ice sheet can form floating icebergs. They are much larger than they look because most of the ice floats below the water surface. Some icebergs may weigh hundreds of thousands of tons.

The basis for life

Many animals, including three quarters of a million whales and other sea mammals, migrate to the Arctic in the summer when the feeding conditions and climate are less hostile. Others spend their whole lives there, supported by the rich food sources of the Arctic Ocean. Food chains start with diatoms, which are types of plant plankton (microscopic organisms that float in the water). The plankton provide ample food for crustaceans and smaller marine animals, which in return support huge schools of fish and shellfish. These are preyed upon by a range of hunters, including seals and walruses.

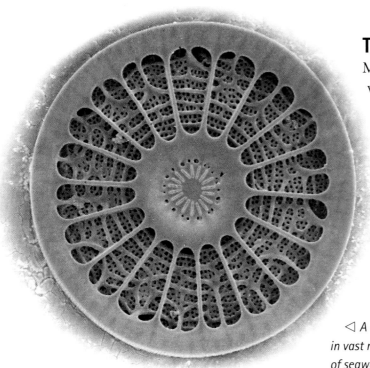

◁ *A diatom viewed under a microscope. Diatoms live in vast numbers in both salt- and freshwater. One glass of seawater can contain more than two million diatoms.*

Walruses and seals

Every summer when the pack ice breaks up and floats around in large chunks, walruses travel with it. They cover up to 3,100 mi. (5,000km) before the winter sets in and the ice locks together again. Walruses use these ice floes as bases from which to hunt mainly shellfish but also snails, worms, and sea cucumbers. They spend most of their life in the sea, surfacing with the aid of air sacs in their throat, which act in a similar way to a life jacket. Some species of seals, such as the ring seal, live deep inside the Arctic Circle. Ring seals hunt fish under the ice, surfacing at small holes in the ice to breathe air. Seals are a vital part of the Arctic food web, because they are eaten by polar bears, killer whales, and walruses.

▽ *Walruses grow up to 14 ft. (4.3m) long and can weigh 2,000 lbs (900kg). They use their 3-ft. (1-m) -long tusks to pull themselves over the ice.*

▽ *Polar bears ambush seals as they surface at breathing holes in the ice. Scavengers such as the Arctic fox may eat the remains of a kill.*

Polar bears

Standing 10 ft. (3m) tall and weighing up to 1,700 lbs (770kg), polar bears are the world's largest land carnivores. They live and breed on the ice but are excellent swimmers, hunting seals and occasionally walruses in the water. Their wide, partially webbed front paws are used as paddles, and they steer with their hind feet. On land they are capable of short bursts of speed of up to 25 mph (40km/h) and are strong enough to smash in the heavy ice roofs that protect young seals in their nurseries. Polar bears rarely drink water—they get most of the moisture they need from seal blubber.

✳ Antarctica

Antarctica is the coldest and windiest place on earth, with winter temperatures as low as –128°F (–89°C) and winds reaching 185 mph (300km/h). The continent only receives about as much water as the Sahara Desert, but it falls as snow. Not all of Antarctica is covered in ice. A range of mountains almost 3,100 mi. (5,000km) long splits it in two, leaving bare rocky outcrops and valleys that support almost no life.

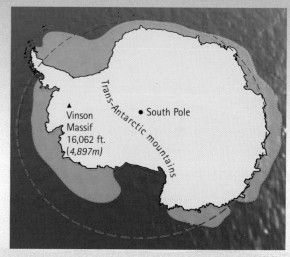

☐ Landmass	⟋ Antarctic Circle
▨ Minimum extent of ice sheet	

△ Pack ice surrounds the Antarctic land mass and extends out into the southern oceans. The ice sheet grows and shrinks with the seasons.

Life on the continent

Antarctica's climate is so severe that little can live permanently on the land. Plant life consists mainly of simple algae, lichens, and mosses. These provide food for some small insects and microorganisms and, closer to the coast, certain seabirds. In contrast to the barren land the seas around Antarctica are teeming with life. Krill, small shrimp like animals that feed on plankton, live in massive swarms. Krill are a major food source for many animals, especially whales.

▽ Krill grow up to 2 in. (5cm) long and live in swarms that can be several miles wide. In some places the krill live so closely together that as many as 20,000 occupy 35 ft³ (1m³).

△ The red tint in this aerial photograph of the McLeod glacier in Antarctica is caused by red snow algae.

Whales

Seals, penguins, and fish all eat krill, but the biggest consumer of all is the whale. A number of species of whales, including the blue whale and the humpback, migrate to Antarctica in the summer especially to eat krill. Krill-eating whales have horny plates in their mouths called baleen plates, which act as a filter. The whale takes a mouthful of seawater and krill, closes its mouth, and forces the water out through the plates with its tongue.

▷ The blue whale is the largest animal on earth. It can measure up to 100 ft. (30m) long and weigh up to 200 tons.

Ashore to breed

Antarctica has no large land predators, making it a safe environment to raise young. Food can only be found on the shore, so most animals that come onto land to breed stay near the coast. Emperor penguins and petrels are two rare exceptions. Albatrosses breed on Antarctic islands where the parents can leave their single chick for days as they hunt for food. Huge elephant seals only come ashore to breed and molt. The males arrive first and fight for space. The females join them, pregnant from the previous year's breeding. The pups are fed on rich milk to build up insulating blubber.

△ The ice fish is unique in the animal kingdom. It is the only vertebrate that does not contain hemoglobin—a substance that helps carry oxygen around the body—in its blood.

Cold seas

Despite the rich supply of food and oxygen, fish struggle to live in the intense cold of the southern oceans. Of the 21,000 species of fish in the world, only 120 can be found in Antarctica, including eel pouts and the Patagonian toothfish. Most of these have chemicals in their blood called glycoproteins. These act as an antifreeze and lower the temperature at which the fish would normally freeze and die.

△ Emperor penguins come ashore in the fall and travel up to 60 mi. (100km) inland to their breeding grounds. The female lays a single egg that the male incubates in a pouch through the winter.

▷ This leopard seal has captured an adlie penguin in the Antarctic waters.

Squid and penguins

Squid are abundant in the waters around the Antarctic. These relatives of the octopus have ten arms and move quickly, propelled by jets of water. Yet they are easy prey for a variety of seabirds, such as penguins and albatrosses. Penguins, in return, are victims of leopard seals. Long, sleek, and fast, the leopard seal confuses a penguin with its rapid movement before using its powerful, wide-hinged jaws to catch the penguin, bite its head and legs off, and then consume its whole body.

People and the Poles

▽ Although the Inuit of today use modern weapons to hunt, they still maintain many of their traditions. Their igloos, built from ice, are temporary shelters used during the winter seal-hunting season.

The two polar regions have had very different histories of contact with humans. The Inuit people have long lived in the Arctic, carefully using its resources, but in the last 150 years modern hunting and industries have exploited more and more of the Arctic tundra. Protected by pack ice, Antartica was untouched by humans at all until 1821, when seal hunters and whalers began to plunder its waters. Today, however, the frozen continent is used purely for scientific research.

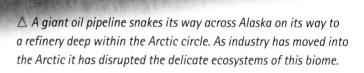

△ A giant oil pipeline snakes its way across Alaska on its way to a refinery deep within the Arctic circle. As industry has moved into the Arctic it has disrupted the delicate ecosystems of this biome.

Inuits and the Arctic

Traditionally the nomadic Inuits lived entirely by hunting, stalking Arctic animals in their kayak canoes and killing them with harpoons. They wasted no resources—their lamps and cooking stoves were powered by blubber, and they used huge whale bones to build their homes, lining them with seal skins for insulation.

Modern Arctic exploitation

European hunters brought disaster to the Inuit. By 1860 more than half their people had been wiped out by European diseases, and since then, their way of life has been steadily eroded. Today many areas of the Arctic are under threat of pollution from giant industrial corporations, which exploit its oil and gas reserves.

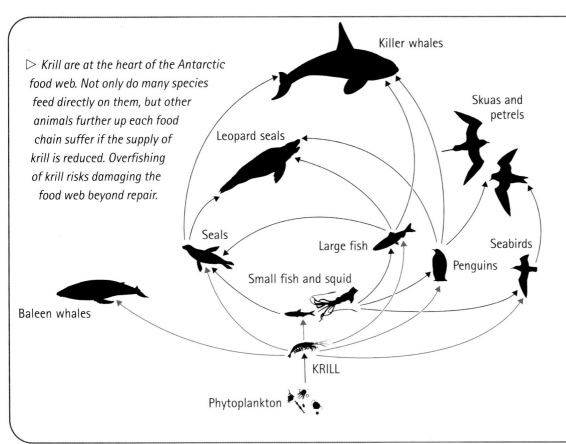

▷ *Krill are at the heart of the Antarctic food web. Not only do many species feed directly on them, but other animals further up each food chain suffer if the supply of krill is reduced. Overfishing of krill risks damaging the food web beyond repair.*

Killer whales

Skuas and petrels

Leopard seals

Seals

Large fish

Seabirds

Penguins

Small fish and squid

Baleen whales

KRILL

Phytoplankton

Modern dangers

Today's threats to the Antarctic biome focus on two key members of the food web. High radiation caused by the growing ozone hole above the Antarctic threatens the floating single-celled plants— phytoplankton—on which the entire biome depends. The huge schools of shrimplike krill, which provide food for much of the Antarctic ecosystem, are also in danger from modern commercial fishing.

Antarctic whaling

The Antarctic biome was most disrupted by whalers in the 1800s and 1900s. They sought valuable baleen plates— the horny plates in many whales' mouths—and oil, which was used for everything from margarine to umbrellas. The whalers mainly hunted blue whales, the biggest of all, shooting them with exploding harpoons. When blue whales were almost wiped out, the hunters turned to fin, sei, and minke whales. In 1988, with many whales on the brink of extinction, the whaling nations agreed to a self-imposed ban. Today whale numbers are increasing slowly, but they still total only 15 percent of the original population. Fortunately this level of disruption has not occurred on land. A few scientists are the only people who have been allowed to settle on the Antarctic landmass.

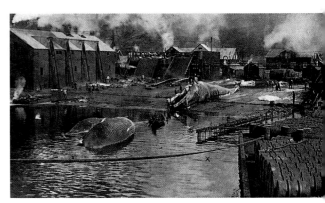

△ *In the early 1900s whaling stations, such as this one on the island of South Georgia, were the center of the industry. With the arrival of factory ships in the 1920s whole whales could be processed at sea, and the speed of slaughter rose quickly. In 1930 alone 30,000 blue whales were killed.*

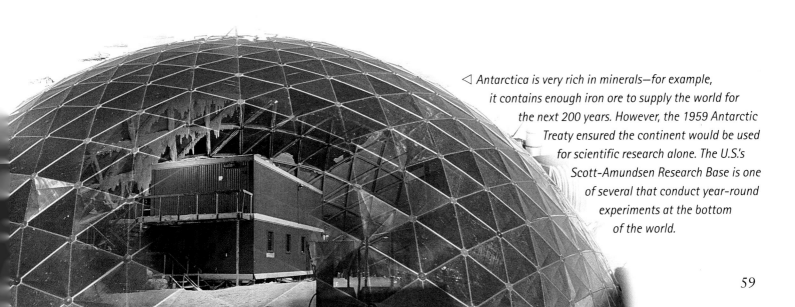

◁ *Antarctica is very rich in minerals—for example, it contains enough iron ore to supply the world for the next 200 years. However, the 1959 Antarctic Treaty ensured the continent would be used for scientific research alone. The U.S.'s Scott-Amundsen Research Base is one of several that conduct year-round experiments at the bottom of the world.*

59

Islands

Islands are isolated landmasses surrounded by water. Many were formed by volcanic activity, causing new land to rise up from the seabed. The Galapagos islands, Iceland, and Tahiti were all created this way. Other islands begin as a coral reef surrounding a volcanic island. The island gradually sinks under the weight of the volcano until all that remains above the surface of the water is a ring-shaped reef of coral known as an atoll.

▽ These are the fruit of the coco de mer, a palm tree unique to the Seychelles Islands in the Indian Ocean. Each fruit takes ten years to mature and can weigh over 50 lbs (22kg).

Special ecosystems

Island ecosystems may vary greatly from those found in mainland areas. Animals that have become extinct in the more competitive environments of the mainland may survive on islands. Isolated from the rest of the world, many island plants and animals have developed into new species that are endemic—or unique to that island. Some island animals shrink in size over generations as the limited resources are better able to support large numbers of smaller creatures. Fossils show that pygmy elephants once lived in the Mediterranean and the East Indies, for example. On islands that lack big predators some species developed into larger versions—giant tortoises and crabs, 10-ft. (3-m) -tall flightless birds and dog-sized rats, for example.

▷ Christmas Island is home to an estimated 100 million red crabs. Every fall, the crabs migrate to the coast to mate and lay their eggs.

Reaching islands

Islands tend to support fewer species than an equivalent area on the mainland because the sea acts as a barrier. Plants and animals overcome this in several ways. Sea mammals and birds have no problem reaching an island, sometimes carrying seeds or insects with them. The seeds of some plants, such as the coconut, can float and are dispersed by the sea. Very light seeds are carried long distances by winds, while small animals and plants reach islands by floating on rafts of vegetation.

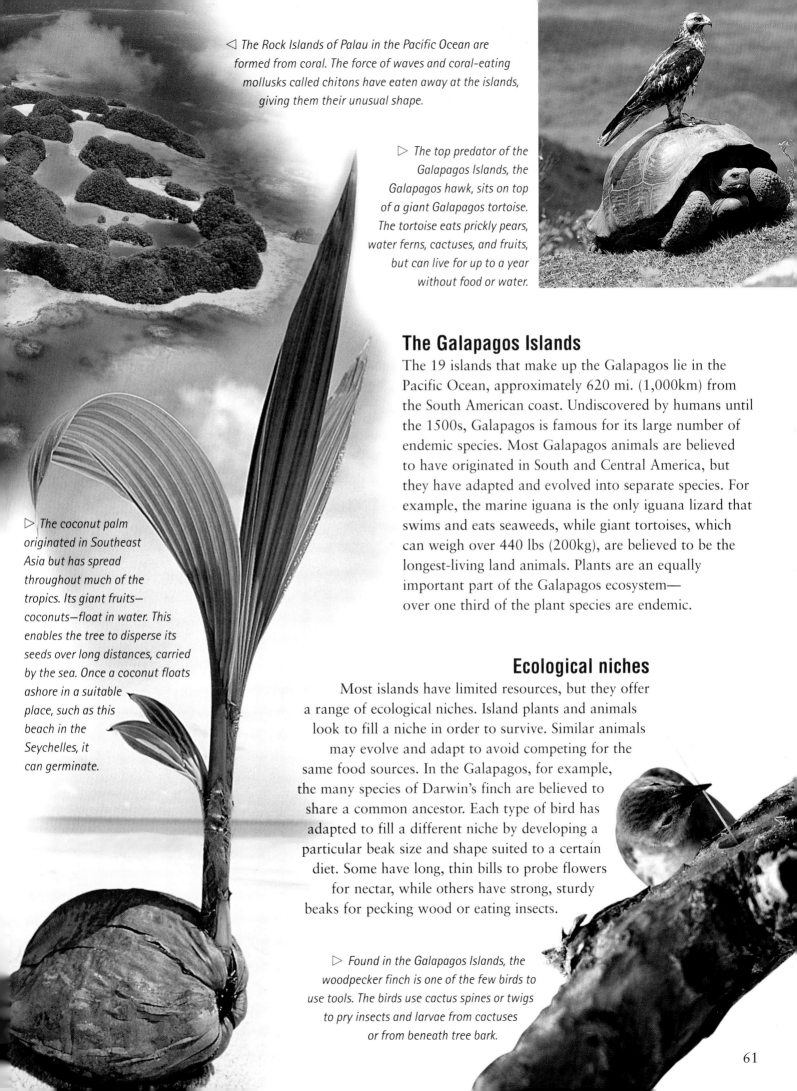

◁ The Rock Islands of Palau in the Pacific Ocean are formed from coral. The force of waves and coral-eating mollusks called chitons have eaten away at the islands, giving them their unusual shape.

▷ The top predator of the Galapagos Islands, the Galapagos hawk, sits on top of a giant Galapagos tortoise. The tortoise eats prickly pears, water ferns, cactuses, and fruits, but can live for up to a year without food or water.

The Galapagos Islands

The 19 islands that make up the Galapagos lie in the Pacific Ocean, approximately 620 mi. (1,000km) from the South American coast. Undiscovered by humans until the 1500s, Galapagos is famous for its large number of endemic species. Most Galapagos animals are believed to have originated in South and Central America, but they have adapted and evolved into separate species. For example, the marine iguana is the only iguana lizard that swims and eats seaweeds, while giant tortoises, which can weigh over 440 lbs (200kg), are believed to be the longest-living land animals. Plants are an equally important part of the Galapagos ecosystem— over one third of the plant species are endemic.

▷ The coconut palm originated in Southeast Asia but has spread throughout much of the tropics. Its giant fruits— coconuts—float in water. This enables the tree to disperse its seeds over long distances, carried by the sea. Once a coconut floats ashore in a suitable place, such as this beach in the Seychelles, it can germinate.

Ecological niches

Most islands have limited resources, but they offer a range of ecological niches. Island plants and animals look to fill a niche in order to survive. Similar animals may evolve and adapt to avoid competing for the same food sources. In the Galapagos, for example, the many species of Darwin's finch are believed to share a common ancestor. Each type of bird has adapted to fill a different niche by developing a particular beak size and shape suited to a certain diet. Some have long, thin bills to probe flowers for nectar, while others have strong, sturdy beaks for pecking wood or eating insects.

▷ Found in the Galapagos Islands, the woodpecker finch is one of the few birds to use tools. The birds use cactus spines or twigs to pry insects and larvae from cactuses or from beneath tree bark.

Large islands

Large islands tend to be formed by volcanic activity, by a rise in sea levels that cuts off a landmass from the mainland, or through continental drift—the moving apart of land continents. Sometimes large islands are created by two of these processes. Australia was initially formed as a result of millions of years of continental drift. Then the partial melting of the polar ice caps about 10,000 years ago caused sea levels to rise, splitting New Zealand and Tasmania from the Australian mainland.

△ Mount Etna, on the large Mediterranean island of Sicily, is Europe's highest volcano and one of the most active in the world. Etna has erupted hundreds of times in recorded history.

Natural arks

Apart from being places where new species evolve, some isolated islands are natural arks. In other words, they preserve descendants that have vanished elsewhere, for example Australia's marsupials—the pouched mammals, such as the kangaroo and koala. The world's fourth largest island, Madagascar in the Indian Ocean, is one of the most ecologically diverse places in the world. It has over 8,000 species of plants, including 1,000 different orchids and more types of palms—175 species—than are found in the entire continent of Africa. Lemurs, tenrecs, two thirds of the world's chameleon species, and many types of nesting birds are found only in Madagascar. Many familiar animals, such as rabbits, moles, monkeys, apes, toads, and newts, are missing. These species never reached the island after it split from Africa.

△ About the size of a domestic cat, the ring-tailed lemur is found only on the large island of Madagascar. It spends up to 40 percent of the day on forest floors, searching for fruit, leaves, flowers, and insects.

Flightless birds

For all of its ecological diversity, Madagascar has only eight species of mammal carnivores—the striped civet, the fossa, and six species of mongooses. Typically, large islands have few large predators, which explains why most of the 40 species of flightless birds still in existence today are found on islands. These include kiwis, takahes, and kakapos in New Zealand and the cassowary of New Guinea and Australia. They evolved from flying ancestors that settled on an island and, with little or no predatory threat, gradually lost their ability to fly. The arrival on many isolated islands of humans, along with introduced predators, such as dogs, posed new threats to many flightless birds. Species including the dodo, from Mauritius, and the 6.5–10-ft. (2–3-m) -tall elephant bird of Madagascar have become extinct in the past 350 years.

Differing habitats

Small islands can offer a range of habitats, from coral reefs to lush woodland groves. Larger islands can feature dozens of habitats and sometimes completely different biomes. Australia, totaling 2.9 million sq. mi. (7.6 million sq. km) of land, has three major biomes. A tropical rain forest is found on the eastern coast, while the center is dominated by huge, dry deserts. Much of the remainder of Australia is savanna grassland. Each biome supports many different habitats, creating thousands of ecological niches for plants and animals to fill.

Australian wildlife

Australia was once part of a supercontinent known as Gondwanaland. Continental drift caused Australia to break away from the mainland, and—over a period of between 55 and 60 million years—move gradually toward its current position. Isolated from evolutionary developments in the rest of the world, Australia has developed its own distinct ecosystems, habitats, and wildlife. In many cases Australian animals are unlike anything found elsewhere in the world.

△ The cassowary, a flightless bird, grows up to 5.75 ft. (1.75m) tall. It eats fruit and dead birds and marsupials in the rain forests of northern Queensland.

Marsupials

Most female mammals have an organ called a placenta. This connects an unborn mammal to its mother's bloodstream, allowing the young to stay inside the mother until it is well developed. Placental mammals colonized earth millions of years ago, but Australia, isolated from the rest of the world, provided a home for older, non-placental mammals. These included marsupials—mammals with pouches— such as the kangaroo, wallaby, koala, bandicoot, and wombat. Like all mammals, marsupials bear live young, but the gestation period inside the mother is very short. Newborn young are very small and weak. For many months after birth they live inside their mother's pouch, suckling milk until they are more developed. Nearly all of Australia's 140 species of marsupials are not found anywhere else in the world.

△ An echidna is a monotreme that eats ants and termites. It tears into mounds or nests with its sharp front claws and pointed snout, catching the insects with its sticky tongue. An echidna does not have teeth. Instead it crushes its prey between spiky pads in its mouth.

▷ A red kangaroo joey weighs little more than 0.04 oz. (1g) at birth and is just 0.8 in. (2cm) long. It remains in its mother's pouch for five to six months and then spends many more months in and out of the pouch before it is fully independent.

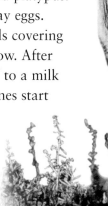

Monotremes

Another group of Australian mammals without a placenta are monotremes, such as the echidna and the duck-billed platypus. Instead of giving birth to live young, monotremes lay eggs. The echidna looks like a hedgehog, with sharp quills covering its body. Female echidnas lay a single egg in a burrow. After it hatches the blind and hairless baby attaches itself to a milk patch on its mother for up to 12 weeks until its spines start to grow. The duck-billed platypus lays two or three eggs in a grass-lined nest. Newly hatched babies are under 0.8 in. (2cm) long, but they eventually grow to an adult size of around 20 in. (50cm).

Australian predators

Despite its large size Australia, like most islands, supports relatively few large predators. Instead of the big wildcats and wolves that exist elsewhere, there are carnivorous marsupials, such as several species of quoll and the Tasmanian devil. About the size of a small dog but incredibly fierce and aggressive, the Tasmanian devil has powerful jaws and teeth capable of cutting through bone. It is one of the few animals that kills and eats its own species. Small mammals, birds, and other animals are hunted by a number of other predators, including birds and venomous snakes. The taipan is believed to be the most deadly snake in the world—an adult carries enough poison to kill 200 sheep.

△ The quoll is a nocturnal, meat-eating marsupial. During the day it hides out in a burrow, a rock pile, or a hollow log. At night it hunts for rats, birds, frogs, rabbits, and insects.

Introduced species

The first known peoples to reach Australia, the Aboriginals arrived over 40,000 years ago. They brought with them a number of nonnative species, including a wild Asian dog called the dingo. From the 1780s on, British and then European settlers introduced a range of new species to Australia. Camels were imported in the 1800s as pack animals for the hot, dry desert interior. Other nonnative species have had a profound impact on Australian ecosystems. Cattle and sheep have altered large grassland areas, while water buffalo have damaged wetland habitats.

The poisonous cane toad and the rabbit, both introduced in small numbers, have multiplied into populations of millions, disrupting fragile natural ecosystems and becoming major agricultural pests.

△ A wild dromedary camel in the Northern Territory of Australia. Today between 60,000 and 90,000 wild camels roam the island's deserts and grasslands.

▷ Dingoes live alone or in small family groups. Their flexible diet includes rats, frogs, injured wallabies, and even fruit. Dingoes' main effect on native ecosystems was to outcompete marsupial carnivores for food. The Tasmanian devil, for example, was once found throughout Australia but is now limited to Tasmania.

People and islands

Since the earliest times, humans have modified or transformed the environments where they live. Islands are no exception. Set apart from mainland areas, smaller islands can especially find their ecosystems dramatically changed by the arrival of human colonists. For example, although islands make up only a small fraction of the total land on earth, approximately one third of the world's plants threatened with extinction grow on islands.

Historic human impact

Easter Island lies in the south Pacific, over 1,860 mi. (3,000km) from any other inhabited land. It is one of the most isolated islands in the world, yet Polynesian voyagers managed to reach it around A.D. 400. The first phase of their impact included introducing chickens, pigs, and certain plants to the island. The second, more destructive phase included their statue-making and overpopulation. At its peak the population of 10,000 people was too great for the island's ecosystem to support. Lush palm forests were destroyed for farmland, firewood, and for devices to help build and carry the statues. Without the forests, soil nutrients were washed away, and many native animals and plants became extinct. The human population shrank as food became scarce, leading to conflicts and even cannibalism.

△ An ancient Moai statue, with its distinctive long nose and deep-set eyes, stands near the coast of Easter Island. Almost 900 of these statues, averaging 13 ft. (4m) in height and 14 tons in weight, were carved out of rock from the sunken volcanic crater at Rano Raraku.

◁ For thousands of years humans have reached islands using simple boats, rafts, and canoes. The Polynesians traveled thousands of miles in canoes with an outrigger, a float that adds stability.

Nonnative species

New species may reach an island in natural ways, such as flying or floating, or be introduced deliberately by humans—sometimes with a profound impact on ecosystems. The native life of the Hawaiian Islands has suffered in this way. The ancient Polynesians brought pigs, chickens, and dogs with them, which hunted and outcompeted certain native animals. The western mosquito fish, introduced more recently to control mosquitoes, has been a major factor in the decline of certain native fish and damselflies. Feral pigs, related to European wild boars, roam parts of Hawaii, killing plants by crushing them or gnawing on their roots.

Human development

As technology has advanced and populations have risen, humans have transformed many island environments. Mediterranean islands, such as Majorca, Ibiza, and Malta, are now major tourist resorts, housing millions. Native plants and animals have suffered from the resulting pollution and habitat destruction. On some islands, such as New Zealand, humans have cleared large forests to grow crops or rear livestock. Mauritius, in the Indian Ocean, was uninhabited by humans until the 1600s, but it is now home to 1.2 million people. Most lowland areas have been cleared to grow crops, and only one percent of native vegetation remains along the island's rivers and volcanic peaks. Mauritius' coral reefs have also suffered, degraded by pollution and dynamite fishing.

△ The mongoose was introduced to Hawaii by European settlers to kill off rats—which were also introduced by humans—in sugar cane fields. Instead the mongoose strayed out of the fields to hunt many species of ground-nesting birds, such as the nene goose.

▽ Human impact at its most extreme used small coral islands in the Pacific as sites to test nuclear weapons. This nuclear test, one of the largest ever, completely destroyed Elugelab Island in 1952.

▽ The humid and rainy climate of the island of Mauritius is perfect for growing sugar cane. Almost all of the island's lowland areas—approximately 85 percent of its total area—have been cleared for sugar cane fields.

Human impact

Urban wildlife

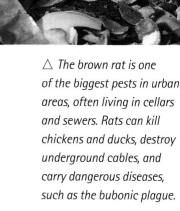

Urban ecosystems cover about 4.5 percent of the world's surface. At a time when many biomes are shrinking, urban environments are greatly expanding as new settlements are created and old ones spread out. Cities have always supported far more life than just humans and their domesticated animals.

Many creatures migrate to and from cities or spend all of their lives there. Some have been deliberately introduced by humans, while others, such as brown rats, were introduced by accident. Animals that can find food and shelter in a variety of ways, known as generalists, are the most likely to flourish in urban areas.

△ The brown rat is one of the biggest pests in urban areas, often living in cellars and sewers. Rats can kill chickens and ducks, destroy underground cables, and carry dangerous diseases, such as the bubonic plague.

△ Marabou storks are African birds. They breed in treetops where they build large nests, but they like to live near human settlements. Adult marabous get much of their food from scavenging. Carrion from a wild animal kill, plowed fields, and garbage dumps are their main sources of food.

Urban homes

Buildings provide animals with a variety of places to seek shelter—from attics inhabited by bats and birds, such as swifts, to the spaces between walls where mice often live. The high ledges of tall buildings are homes to starlings and sparrows, as well as cliff-nesting birds such as gulls and kestrels. A city's infrastructure— its transportation, water, power, and sewer systems— provide many opportunities for shelter. Bats may make their homes in ventilation shafts, while underground transportation systems and sewers provide shelter for rats, mice, and many insects.

▷ The ledges and roofs of tall city buildings make a home for a range of birds, such as this herring gull and its chick.

▷ Many animals seek shelter from the cold or blistering sun inside buildings. Food, in the form of insects, attracts small predators like these geckos on a ceiling in Southeast Asia.

Heat islands

Many animals are drawn to and flourish in urban environments. One reason is that cities and towns tend to be "heat islands." This means they have higher temperatures than the surrounding country. Rivers and canals are more likely to be ice-free, which provides extra feeding opportunities for birds.

Garbage

Waste dumps in urban areas let off heat as they decompose. This provides a sufficient habitat for some cold-blooded reptiles, like slow-worms and small lizards. Humans generate a huge amount of organic waste. Left on city streets, in trash cans, and at dumps, this is a huge food resource for insects, small reptiles, birds such as crows and gulls, and foxes, possums, rats, and other scavenging mammals.

▽ The green spaces of a town or city provide vital habitats for many different species, such as these common frogs in an urban pond in Great Britain.

Challenges to life

An urban environment also poses challenges to life. Food, sunlight, and space to live and breed are limited in many cities, while the threat of vehicles and pest controls can restrict population numbers. Pollution, particularly from vehicles, means that wildlife has to cope with on average ten times more dust particles and carbon dioxide and 25 times more carbon monoxide than in the surrounding country. Despite these tough conditions, many cities support a large and often diverse range of life.

▽ Close to one million alligators live in Florida, many of them in Everglades National Park. Occasionally alligators may stray into urban areas, but they are only dangerous if provoked.

Pests and threats

Many animals that live in towns and cities are seen as pests that must be controlled. Some carry diseases—raccoons, for example, are prone to rabies. Others, such as pigeons, exist in huge numbers due to a lack of natural predators. Some animals lose their natural habitats as cities grow outward. They have little choice but to try to survive on the fringes of the urban environment. Larger mammals, such as coyotes in North America, jackals in Africa and Asia, the opossum in Oceania, and the fox in Europe, live as scavengers on domestic waste and will occasionally attack pets or backyard wildlife.

A world transformed

Early humans were controlled by their environment. They hunted wild animals, gathered plants, and many lived as nomads, wandering to places where food was available. As people learned to farm they began to have much more impact on ecosystems. This impact has increased greatly with the growth of cities and the manufacturing industry and advances in technology. Today much of the world's landscape has been transformed, and its natural cycles have been altered to meet human demands.

△ Pesticides, such as those being sprayed over farmland by this helicopter, are chemicals designed to kill certain insects, weeds, or fungi that are considered pests. Many pesticides kill other living things in addition to the original target. Today fewer pesticides are used, and many are designed so that they will be broken down quickly and naturally.

Feeding six billion

In 1700 there were approximately 200 million people on the planet. By 1971 the world population had risen to 3.8 billion. Just 30 years later it broke the six billion mark. With this massive increase in mouths to feed have come radical new farming processes. Many of these generate more food but also have a major impact on ecosystems. In certain places the heavy use of fertilizers has overloaded the nitrogen cycle, causing nitrates to contaminate groundwater. Massive fields, created by clearing woodlands and ponds, are often used to grow a single species (a monoculture). In response, many people are demanding more organic farming, where foods are grown without heavy chemicals and in a way that allows wild plants and animals to flourish.

Shrinking ecosystems

The pressure to feed the growing world population has been a key reason why many ecosystems are shrinking and disappearing. Modern agriculture is often conducted on a large scale, with grasslands and forests destroyed to make room for grazing and crops. Other pressures stem from mining and manufacturing, which pollute ecosystems, and from towns and cities that have sprawled into the country, fragmenting what remains of habitats. The combined impact of these human-driven developments is devastating—almost two thirds of Europe's and half of the United States' wetlands have been drained, while around 45 percent of the world's forests have been cut down in the last 40 years.

◁ Large parts of the Amazon rain forest have been destroyed to make room for cattle ranching. The soil can only support the grazing of cattle for a few years.

Controlling nature

Humans use tools and technology to massively change the world around them—from damming rivers and creating artificial lakes and beaches to reclaiming land from the sea. Recently scientists have begun to alter the genetic makeup of living things. Genetically modified (GM) species contain genes taken from other species to improve certain characteristics—such as making a plant crop more resistant to frost or pests. Those in favor of genetically modified food believe that it will produce a food boom, with fewer crops lost to disease and bad weather. Some opponents of genetic engineering think that humans shouldn't try to "play god" by tampering with nature in this way. Others fear that GM crops could spread into the wider environment and introduce their genes into wild plant varieties. This could produce superweeds that are resistant to pesticides.

△ One of the world's biggest construction projects, Hong Kong's Chek Lap Kok Airport, opened in 1998. It covers 482 sq. mi. (1,248 sq km), with one quarter of the site built on existing islands. The other three quarters, equivalent to over 1,200 football fields, consists of land reclaimed from the sea.

◁ Bucardo mountain goats lived in the Pyrenees mountains of northern Spain until the last remaining goat died in 2000. Scientists had taken cells from the goat before its death. Using genetic engineering, they intend to clone the cells and produce an embyro that can be implanted into another species of goat. The hope is that new young can be born and the species brought back from extinction.

Protest

Concerns about the ways in which humans are transforming the planet have led to the rise of environmental pressure groups and organizations. These lobby governments and manufacturing industries for change. They also raise public awareness of problems—from the plight of endangered species to global warming—by sponsoring scientific research, publishing reports, and sometimes protesting. In several countries, particularly in Europe, environmentally concious, or "Green," political parties have won many votes. They campaign for bans on poaching, for more sustainable methods of producing energy and food, and for cutbacks in pollution. Certain reforms have taken place. These include greater use of renewable energy, laws to reduce polluting emissions from motor vehicles, and the banning of CFCs—types of gases previously used in refrigerators and aerosol cans—that damage the ozone layer and contribute to the greenhouse effect.

▽ Environmental organizations, such as Greenpeace, have campaigned to stop commercial whaling from further reducing the number of whales in the world's oceans. Here, Greenpeace activists stage a nonviolent protest by confronting a whaling vessel.

Human impact

🌍 The future

Earth is naturally dynamic. Its continents shift, its climates change, and natural forces—from volcanic activity to shore erosion—reshape the planet. Many species adapt to these natural changes over millions of years, while others die out, making room for new species to evolve. However, it is much more difficult for species to adapt to the rapid changes caused by humans in recent centuries. The future may see more and more species becoming extinct, biological diversity reduced, and possibly a major climatic shift for the entire planet.

△ At the start of the 1900s there were an estimated 100,000 tigers in the wild. Habitat loss and poaching by humans has seen that number plummet to below 10,000.

Extinction

Extinction is the end of an evolutionary line with the death of the final member of a species. Many millions of species have become extinct since earth first supported life. Extinction is a natural event believed to be vital in the process of evolution—where new species come to prominence and other, older species die out—but the current rate of extinction is worryingly high.

Most of the extinctions that have occurred in the past 300 years have been caused by humans. In North America, for example, over 400 species of plants and animals have become extinct since humans settled there. Thousands more species are in danger of extinction unless their habitats are conserved and the threats to their survival, from pollution to poaching, are removed.

▽ These young spur-tailed tortoises are part of a breeding program at the Tortoise Village in Gonfaron, France. The center, home to more than 1,500 animals, was set up in 1988 to study and protect tortoises and turtles and their habitats.

◁ African elephants and impalas gather around a water hole in the relative safety of Chobe National Park in Botswana, Africa. The park, 4,520 sq. mi. (11,700 sq km) in area, contains over 450 bird species and supports the highest concentration of elephants in Africa.

Biodiversity

Earth is home to at least 14 million species of living things. This incredible variety supports humankind's own existence by providing food, fuel, building materials, medicine, and raw materials with which to make other products. Biological diversity—or biodiversity for short—also helps buffer ecosystems from sudden change and provides "natural services" such as clean air, clean water, and the removal of decaying matter. With larger numbers of extinctions comes a reduction in biodiversity and the possibility that some of these natural services will not be carried out as efficiently.

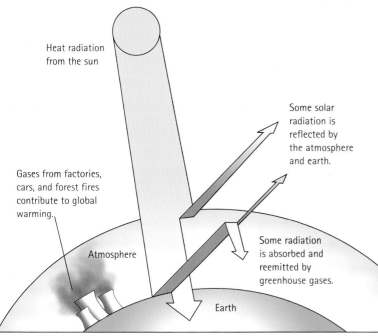

Heat radiation from the sun

Some solar radiation is reflected by the atmosphere and earth.

Gases from factories, cars, and forest fires contribute to global warming.

Atmosphere

Some radiation is absorbed and reemitted by greenhouse gases.

Earth

Climate change

One of the biggest threats to the future well-being of the planet may come from changes in the climates of many biomes. The world is warming up faster than at any time in the last 10,000 years, with the 1990s being the hottest decade since detailed records were kept. Much of this climate change is believed to be a result of the greenhouse effect, where more gases that trap the sun's energy are emitted into earth's atmosphere. Many experts believe that ecosystems and living things are under threat from global warming. An average temperature rise of 36°F (2°C) would prevent some farmlands from supporting crops, could lead to an increase in floods, droughts, forest fires, and coral decay, and could see many species of plants and animals disappear from certain habitats.

△ Gases in the atmosphere naturally trap some of the sun's energy, helping to keep the planet warm. Additional greenhouse gases, emitted by manufacturing plants, vehicles, and other human activities, trap more of the sun's energy and are believed to be the major reason why earth is heating up.

▽ One consequence of global temperature rises could be more flooding. This is the swollen Tana river, in Kenya.

▷ Scientists predict that earth's temperature could rise between about 34°F (1°C) (the dotted line) and 37°F (3°C) (the solid line) by 2070. This would be a steep rise from 20th-century levels (see graph).

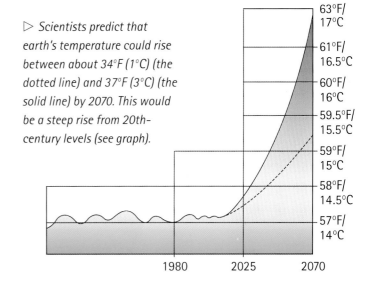

63°F/ 17°C
61°F/ 16.5°C
60°F/ 16°C
59.5°F/ 15.5°C
59°F/ 15°C
58°F/ 14.5°C
57°F/ 14°C

1980   2025   2070

▷ Located in a china clay pit in Cornwall, England, the Eden Project houses thousands of plant species in different climatic zones. This is part of the humid tropic biome.

Conservation

Traditionally the aim of conservation was to save single threatened species. In some cases the population of an endangered species is so small that animals are taken out of the wild and placed in captive breeding programs. The goal is to increase their numbers in a safe environment before returning the animals to the wild. Today conservation also aims to preserve habitats and entire ecosystems. As the human population grows and increases its ability to transform environments, the survival of individual species and entire ecosystems will depend more and more on humans finding ways to conserve the planet's resources or use them in a sustainable way.

Classification of living things

Millions of species

There may be more than 14 million different species of life on earth. Only around 1.75 million have been identified so far. Classification and naming systems allow people to identify and compare different living things. They help scientists around the globe study and understand the natural world and relate types of living things to species that died out long ago. The first stage of classification divides the millions of species into five kingdoms—animals, plants, fungi, monerans, and protists.

▽ *The first stage of classification divides the natural world into five kingdoms.*

Animals (over one million species)
Many-celled, usually mobile organisms that are heterotrophic—unable to generate food from direct energy sources. They live by eating plants and other animals.

Plants (over 250,000 species)
Many-celled organisms that are autotrophic—capable of producing their own food through the process of photosynthesis.

Fungi (over 50,000 species)
Organisms which obtain nutrients by absorbing food. Fungi reproduce by making spores.

Monerans (over 4,000 species)
Split into two types: true bacteria (or eubacteria) and archaebacteria. Most monerans are single-celled, microscopic organisms. They usually get their energy from substances around them, although some monerans use photosynthesis.

Protists (over 50,000 species)
Mainly single-celled (but sometimes many-celled) organisms, including amoebas and protozoa.

Scientific names

Biologists and naturalists use a naming system invented by the Swedish botanist, Carolus Linnaeus, where plants and animals are given Latin names. These names have two parts. The first word identifies the genus to which the organism belongs, and the second word is the name of its actual species. For example, the gray wolf (*Canis lupus*) is part of the genus *Canis* (which includes jackals, some wolves, and the dingo), and its species name is *lupus*.

▽ *Plants can be divided into different groups according to how they reproduce.*

Flowering plants (240,000 species)
Monocotyledons (tulips, for example) produce seeds with a single leaf. Dicotyledons (sunflowers, for example) have seeds with two leaves.

Cone-bearing plants (500 species)
Conifers and related plants produce their seeds on woody cones.

Spore-producing plants (26,000 species)
Ferns usually reproduce through spores on the underside of their leaves. Mosses and liverworts usually produce their spores in a capsule on a stalk.

From kingdom to species

The differences in the structure of an organism's cells partly determine to which of the five kingdoms the organism belongs. There are a number of phyla (groups of living things that have a similar body plan or organization) within each kingdom. Each phylum is divided into one or more classes. Each class is split into orders, which are divided into families and then genera. The smallest complete group is an individual species.

▽ *The scientific name for the honeybee is* Apis mellifera.

Kingdom—Animalia (animals)
▼
Phylum—Arthropoda (joint-footed animals)
▼
Class—Insecta (insects)
▼
Order—Hymenoptera (bees, ants, and wasps)
▼
Family—Apidae (bumblebees and honeybees)
▼
Genus—Apis
▼
Species—mellifera

Further resources

Websites

www.bbsr.edu/agcihome/sitelinks/globalchange.html
A large collection of links to webpages concerned with environmental and climate change.

www.biodiversity911.org
Webpages devoted to the issue of biodiversity, with many links to other living world sites.

www.edenproject.com
The website of the giant collection of plants, opened in Cornwall, England, in 2001. The site includes a virtual tour and features about biodiversity and conservation.

www.eelink.net/EndSpp
A website that charts the many endangered species of plants and animals around the world.

www.eppresents.com/VirtualLibrary/Biomes/biomespage.htm
A large, accessible collection of features and images about the world's major biomes.

www.fao.org/desertification
A United Nations' website on the topic of desertification, including maps, images, and news.

www.foei.org
Friends of the Earth International is a worldwide collection of groups campaigning for the protection of wildlife and habitats.

www.greenpeace.org
The homepage of Greenpeace International, which runs campaigns and direct action to defend the environment.

www.nationalgeographic.com
The website of *National Geographic* magazine, with features on animals, plants, habitats, and regions.

www.noaa.gov
The homepage of the United States National Oceanic and Atmospheric Administration (NOAA), containing information about coastlines, coral reefs, and ocean life.

www.nsf.gov/od/opp/wwwsites.htm
A long list of bookmarks and hyperlinks to sites about the Arctic and Antarctic polar regions.

www.panda.org/resources/publications/sustainability/ indigenous/proj_brazil.htm
This website examines the challenges facing many indigenous peoples all over the world.

www.pbs.org/tal/costa_rica/rainfacts.html
A website devoted to the science of the rain forest, packed full of interesting facts and features.

www.survival-international.org
Survival International works to protect native tribes and peoples and the environments in which they live.

www.wildlifer.com/wildlifesites
A large collection of categorized links to websites devoted to all forms of wildlife.

www.worldwildlife.org
The Worldwide Fund for Nature campaigns for animal, plant, and habitat protection across the globe.

Books

The Blue Planet, Andrew Byatt et al., BBC Consumer Publishing, 2001.

Deserts, Philip Steele, Zoe Books Limited, 1996.

Facts on File: Environment Atlas, David Wright, Facts on File, 1997.

The Gaia Atlas of Planet Management, Norman Myers (editor) and Gerald Durrell, Oxfam Books, 1994.

The Guinness Book of Amazing Nature, Elizabeth Wyse (managing editor), Guinness Publishing, 1998.

An Introduction to the World's Oceans, Alison B. Duxbury, McGraw-Hill, 1996.

Journey to the Rain Forest, Tim Knight, Oxford, 2002.

The Kingfisher Book of Evolution, Stephen Webster, Kingfisher Publications, 2000.

The Kingfisher Book of Oceans, David Lambert, Kingfisher Publications, 1997.

Landmark Geography: Ecosystems and Human Activity, Julia Woodfield, Collins Educational, 2000.

Nature's Predators, Michael Bright, Barbara Taylor, and Robin Kerrod, Southwater, 1991.

World Atlas of Coral Reefs, Mark D. Spalding, Corinna Ravilious and Edmund P. Green, University of California Press, 2001.

Glossary

Acid rain Rain and snow that contains poisonous or harmful acidic chemicals—such as sulfur dioxide, which is created by burning coal, oil, and gas.

Adaptation A change in the structure or behavior of an organism that makes it more able to live in a particular environment.

Algae Plantlike organisms that contain chlorophyll but have no actual leaves or roots.

Atoll A ring-shaped island made of coral reef that surrounds a lagoon.

Bacteria Microscopic, single-celled organisms. Bacteria are the most abundant living things on earth.

Biodiversity The variety of species in a particular area.

Biome A large, general habitat covering a region of earth. Tundra, boreal forests, deserts, and grasslands are all biomes.

Biosphere The parts of earth where living things exist.

Blubber A thick layer of fat that helps keep some animals warm. Polar bears, seals, whales, and penguins all have blubber.

Camouflage The way that the coloring and markings of an animal blend in with its surroundings, making the animal difficult to see.

Carnivore An animal or plant that eats meat.

Carrion The rotting flesh of dead animals often eaten by scavengers.

Cartilage A tough, flexible tissue in the skeleton of a vertebrate. It can form parts of the body such as the nose and ears. In cartilaginous fish, such as sharks, it forms the entire skeleton.

Cell A tiny unit of living matter. Cells are the building blocks of all living things.

Chlorophyll The green chemical in a plant that traps the energy in sunlight. Plants use this energy to make food.

Climate The general weather conditions of a region over a long period of time.

Conifer A plant that reproduces by making cones. Conifers are mainly evergreen trees and bushes that keep their leaves all year long.

Deciduous Deciduous trees shed their leaves every fall. This helps them conserve water throughout the winter.

Decomposer A living thing that gains nutrients by breaking down dead plant and animal matter. The minerals contained in the dead matter are released into the environment.

Deforestation The cutting down of large numbers of trees for fuel or timber or to use the land for communities or farming.

Desertification The way a desert expands and spreads, reducing the land's ability to support life. Desertification is caused by climate changes, overfarming, overgrazing, and by removing plants that hold the soil in place.

Digest To break down food so that it can be absorbed and used by the body.

Domesticated animal An animal that is kept as a pet, a means of transportation or for food, rather than one living in the wild.

Dormant Inactive, hibernating, or not growing.

Ecology The branch of science that studies the relationships between different living things and their environments.

Ecosystem A collection of all the living things and their nonliving surroundings in a particular area.

Embryo A tiny bundle of cells that makes up a young plant or animal in the earliest stage of its development.

Endangered species Species of living things that are seriously threatened with extinction.

Enzymes A substance that speeds up the processes that take place inside a living thing. For example, digestive enzymes change food into liquids that can enter the blood and travel around the body.

Epiphyte A plant that grows on another plant or on a rock instead of in the soil. Epiphytes obtain moisture and nutrients directly from the air.

Equator The imaginary line around the center of earth, an equal distance from the North and South poles.

Evaporation The process by which a liquid changes into a gas. For example, the warming of air by sunlight causes water in plants to evaporate and change into water vapor.

Evolution The long-term process of change in organisms, often taking place over millions of years.

Extinction The permanent disappearance of a species with the death of its last member.

Feral A feral species is one that was once domesticated but has since returned to live in the wild.

Fertilization The process by which a male and female cell join together to form an embryo.

Fertilizer A substance added to soil to make it more fertile.

Food chain A food chain shows the links between different animals that eat plants and one another. Energy and nutrients pass up through the chain. Large carnivores, such as eagles and wildcats, tend to be at the top of food chains, with plants and decomposers at the bottom.

Food web A diagram showing all the interconnected food chains in an ecosystem.

Gene The part of a cell that passes characteristics—such as eye or hair color—from an adult to its offspring.

Genetic engineering Changing the genes in a living cell so that the cell can do something it could not do naturally.

Germination The first stage in the growth of a seed or spore into a plant.

Gill The part of an aquatic animal's body that collects oxygen from the water and enables the animal to breathe.

Greenhouse effect The build-up of certain gases such as carbon dioxide and methane in earth's atmosphere. The gases trap the sun's heat and affect earth's climate.

Habitat The surroundings that a particular species needs to survive. Habitats include coral reefs, grasslands, lakes, and deserts. Some species can live in more than one habitat.

Hemisphere One half of earth's sphere above or below the equator. Seasons in the Southern Hemisphere are the opposite of those in the Northern Hemisphere.

Herbivore An animal that eats only plants.

Hibernation A deep sleep, usually in the winter, which enables some animals to survive when food is hard to find.

Host An animal that a parasite uses as its home and food source.

Humus A substance found in the soil made from dead plant and animal matter. Humus helps keep soil fertile.

Incubate To keep eggs warm by sitting on them.

Insulation A layer of fur, fat, or feathers that reduces the amount of heat lost from an animal's body.

Introduced species A species that people have taken from one part of the world and released into another area. Introduced species can have devastating consequences on the ecosystems into which they are released.

Invertebrate An animal without a backbone, such as an insect, a worm, or a snail.

Irrigation A system of watering land by using pipes and ditches to channel water.

Krill Small, shrimplike animals that exist in the millions in polar seas. They provide food for whales, fish, and other animals.

Larva The young form of an insect, which looks very different from an adult. A caterpillar is the larva of a butterfly.

Leaf litter The layer of whole leaves and leaf fragments that carpets the floor of a forest.

Life cycle All the major stages in the life of an organism—from the start of its life through to its growth, and breeding, and finally death.

Microclimate The climate of a small, defined area, such as a valley.

Migration Round trips made by animals between habitats in search of food or to reach breeding grounds. Many animals, including wildebeest and birds, migrate every year.

Mineral A chemical substance, such as iron or magnesium, that occurs naturally in rocks and soil. All plants and animals need certain minerals in order to survive.

Niche A place that something can fit into. An ecological niche is the way in which a living thing fits into its environment.

Nocturnal Active mainly at night.

Nomad An animal or human that does not have a fixed home and usually keeps on the move, traveling to wherever food can be found.

Nutrient Material taken in by a living thing to help it stay alive.

Omnivore An animal that eats both plants and animals.

Organism Any living thing.

Parasite An organism that feeds on or inside another living thing, which is called the host. Parasites are usually much smaller than their hosts and don't always harm them.

Permafrost Ground that is permanently frozen, such as the soil below the surface of the tundra.

Pesticide A chemical used by farmers that kills pests—animals that damage crops or livestock.

Photosynthesis The process by which plants use the energy from sunlight to make food from water and carbon dioxide.

Plankton Microscopic living things that drift near the surface of lakes and oceans. Plankton includes algae, which collect energy from sunlight, and tiny animals that eat algae or each other.

Pollen A dustlike powder, produced by plants that contains male sex cells.

Pollination The movement of pollen from the male part of a flower to the female part so that reproduction can occur.

Predator An animal that kills and then eats another animal, which is known as its prey.

Prehensile Able to grip or grasp an object. Some monkeys have a prehensile tail, which they use to grip branches as they swing through the canopy of a rain forest.

Prey An animal that is hunted and killed for food.

Pupate When an insect larva pupates, it makes a tough case around its body. Protected by the case, the larva changes shape and becomes an adult.

Reproduction The production of a new living thing by an organism.

Respiration Breathing.

Scavenger An animal, such as a vulture or a hyena, which feeds on the dead remains of animals or plants.

Soil erosion The process by which loose soil is washed or blown away.

Species A set of organisms that can be grouped together due to their similarity and their ability to breed with each other.

Symbiosis A close relationship between two organisms of different species. Sometimes both species benefit, but in many partnerships one species gains much more than the other.

Temperate Neither very hot nor very cold. Temperate zones lie between the tropics and the polar regions.

Territory The area in which an animal lives and finds food. Animals often defend their territory against other members of the same species.

Tributary A stream or river that flows into a larger river or a lake.

Tropics The region around the equator that remains hot all year round.

Vertebrate An animal that has a backbone.

Index

Acknowledgments

The publishers would like to thank the following for providing photographs:

Front cover Still Pictures/GAYO, *c* National Geographic Society/Annie Griffiths Bell, *cl* www.osf.uk.com/Raymond J. C. Cannon, *t* www.osf.uk.com/Michael Sewell; **back cover** *b* Bruce Coleman Collection/Staffan Widstrand.

Page 6 *c* Still Pictures/Klein/Hubert, *cr* www.osf.uk.com/Paul Kay; **6-7** *br* NHPA/ A.N.T.; **7** *cl* BBC Natural History Unit Picture Library/Sue Flood, *c* Ardea London/Jean-Paul Ferrero; **8** *r* www.osf.uk.com/Neil Bromhall, *bl* Still Pictures/Fritz Polking; **9** *tl* www.osf.uk.com/Satoshi Kuribayashi, *cr* Ardea London/John Clegg, *b* Ardea London/ P. Morris; **10** *tr* www.osf.uk.com/Norbert Wu, *cl* www.osf.uk.com/Paulo De Oliveira; **11** *tr* Frank Lane Picture Agency/Fritz Polking, *cl* www.osf.uk.com/James H. Robinson, *br* BBC Natural History Unit Picture Library/Anup Shah; **12** *bl* Corbis/Alissa Crandall; **13** *cl* NHPA/ B. Jones & M. Shimlock, *c* Still Pictures/Volker Steger, *br* NHPA/Guy Edwards; **14** *c* Ardea London/Pat Morris, *bl* Corbis/Jeffrey L. Rotman; **14-15** *tc* Ardea London/François Gohier, *bc* BBC Natural History Unit Picture Library/David Shale; **15** *tr* Corbis/Ralph White, *br* www.osf.uk.com/ Scripps Inst. Oceanography; **16** *cl* Frank Lane Picture Agency/Silvestris, *bl* NHPA/B. Jones & M. Shimlock, *bc* Bruce Coleman Collection/Pacific Stock; **17** *tc* Ardea London/Ron & Valerie Taylor, *tr* Ardea London/Kurt Amsler, *bl* Bruce Coleman Collection/Natural Selection Inc., *br* Bruce Coleman Collection/Franco Banfi; **18** *tr* Ardea London/Bob Gibbons, *cl* BBC Natural History Unit Picture Library/Niall Benvie, *bc* BBC Natural History Unit Picture Library/Jeff Foott; **18-19** BBC Natural History Unit Picture Library/ T. Andrewartha, *c* Ardea London/Hans D. Dossenbach; **19** *tl* Ardea London/Valerie Taylor, *cl* NHPA/Dr Ivan Polunin; **20** *tr* Ardea London/ John Daniels, *bl* NHPA/Silvestris Fotoservice, *br* www.osf.uk.com/Okapia; **20-21** *c* Ardea London/ Adrian Warren; **21** *tl* Ardea London, *cr* Ardea London/François Gohier, *br* www.osf.uk.com/ Andrew Plumptre; **22** *tr* www.osf.uk.com/NASA, *bl* Corbis/Carl Purcell; **23** *tl* Ardea London/David & Katie Urry, *c* Ardea London/François Gohier, *br* www.osf.uk.com/Mary Plage; **24** *tr* BBC Natural History Unit Picture Library/David Noton, *cl* Still Pictures/Ronald Seitre; **24-25** *b* Still Pictures/Ronald Seitre; **25** *cl* Ardea London/ François Gohier, *br* Ardea London/François Gohier; **26** *cr* www.osf.uk.com/G. I. Bernard, *bl* Bruce Coleman Collection/Natural Selection Inc.; **26-27** *t* Science Photo Library/Gregory Dimijian, *c* Ardea London/Masahiro Lijima;

27 *tr* www.osf.uk.com/Michael Sewell, *cr* Frank Lane Picture Agency/J. Zimmermann, *bl* Science Photo Library/Fletcher & Baylis; **28** *tr* www.osf.uk.com/Mike Linley, *bl* Ardea London/J. P. Ferrero; **29** *tl* Still Pictures/Alain Compost, *tr* Frank Lane Picture Agency, *cl* Ardea London/M. D. England, *br* BBC Natural History Unit Picture Library/Phil Savoie; **30** *tr* Ardea London/Eric Dragesco, *cl* Ardea London/Martin W. Grosnick, *cr* Ardea London/M. Watson; **30-31** *b* BBC Natural History Unit Picture Library/ Andrew Zvoznikov; **31** *tl* Ardea London/J. A. Bailey, *tl* Ardea London/John Swedberg, *cl* Ardea London/Dennis Avon, *cr* NHPA/Stephen Dalton; **32** *tr* NHPA/Stephen Dalton, *cl* Ardea London/ François Gohier, *b* www.osf.uk.com/David M. Dennis; **32-33** Still Pictures/Alex S. Maclean; **33** *tr* Ardea London/J. Swedberg, *cr* NHPA/ A. N. T., *bl* Ardea London/Bob Gibbons; **34** *tr* Ardea London/Bill Coster, *cl* Corbis/Arne Hodalic, *b* www.osf.uk.com/Chris Sharp; **35** *tl* Frank Lane Picture Agency/Silvestris Fotoservice, *c* NHPA/Martin Harvey, *br* Ardea London/ Jean-Paul Ferrero; **36** *tr* Ardea London/Ferrero-Labat, *cl* Ardea London/Ferrero-Labat, *cr* Ardea London/Ferrero-Labat; **36-37** *b* BBC Natural History Unit Picture Library/T. Andrewartha; **37** *tr* www.osf.uk.com/Steve Turner, *cl* www.osf.uk.com/Martyn Colbeck; **38** *cr* BBC Natural History Unit Picture Library/Anup Shah, *b* Bruce Coleman Collection/HPH Photography; **39** *tr* NHPA/Christopher Ratier, *cl* BBC Natural History Unit Picture Library/Anup Shah, *b* BBC Natural History Unit Picture Library/Peter Blackwell; **40** *tr* Bruce Coleman Collection, *cl* Ardea London/François Gohier; **40-41** Bruce Coleman Collection; **41** *tl* BBC Natural History Unit Picture Library/Jeff Foott, *br* BBC Natural History Unit Picture Library/John Downer; **42** *tr* Ardea London/Wendy Shattil/Bob Rozinski, *cl* Ardea London/Adrian Warren, *br* Corbis/ Bettmann; **43** *tl* Frank Lane Picture Agency/ Gerard Lacz, *cr* Corbis/Kit Houghton, *b* BBC Natural History Unit Picture Library/Pete Oxford; **44** *tr* NASA, *br* Corbis; **44-45** *b* Frank Lane Picture Agency/David Hosking; **45** *tr* Ardea London/François Gohier, *cl* NASA, *br* Still Pictures/Frans Lemmens; **46** *tr* www.osf.uk.com/ Michael Fogden, *cl* NHPA/Rod Planck, *br* Ardea London/Peter Steyn; **47** *tr* Ardea London/Peter Steyn, *c* www.osf.uk.com/Michael Fogden, *cr* www.osf.uk.com/Avril Ramage, *br* NHPA/Dave Watts; **48** *tr* Still Pictures/John Cancalosi, *cl* www.osf.uk.com/Tim Jackson, *bl* Corbis; **49** *tr* Corbis, *cl* Frank Lane Picture Agency/L. W. Walker, *br* BBC Natural History Unit Picture Library/Graham Hatherley; **50** *cl* Still Pictures/ UNEP, *cr* Corbis; **50-51** BBC Natural History Unit Picture Library/Pete Oxford; **51** *cl* Corbis,

bl www.osf.uk.com/C. W. Helliwell, *br* NASA; **52** *tr* Still Pictures/Thomas D. Mangelsen, *cr* Still Pictures/Gunter Ziesler, *bl* Still Pictures/ Kim Heacox; **52-53** *b* BBC Natural History Unit Picture Library/Staffan Widstrand; **53** *tl* Ardea London/Andrey Zvoznikov, *tr* Bruce Coleman Collection/Gordon Langsbury, *cr* Still Pictures/ Thomas D. Mangelsen; **54** *cr* Corbis/Amos Nachoum, *b* Ardea London/E. Mickleburgh; **55** *tl* Corbis/Jim Zuckerman, *cr* BBC Natural History Unit Picture Library/Doc White, *bl* BBC Natural History Unit Picture Library/Tom Mangelsen; **56** *cl* BBC Natural History Unit Picture Library/ Doug Allan, *cr* www.osf.uk.com/Rudie H. Kuiter, *br* BBC Natural History Unit Picture Library/ Doc White; **56-57** BBC Natural History Unit Picture Library/Martha Holmes; **57** *tl* NHPA/ Norbert Wu, *tr* Ardea London/C. G. Robertson, *b* www.osf.uk.com/Doug Allan; **58** *tr* Bruce Coleman Collection/Staffan Widstrand, *cl* NHPA/ B. & C. Alexander, *c* Corbis; **59** *cr* The Royal Geographical Society/A. C. Hardy, *bl* The Royal Geographical Society/Charles Swithinbank, *bc* The Royal Geographical Society/Charles Swithinbank; **60** *cl* www.osf.uk.com/John Brown, *br* Ardea London/Jean-Paul Ferrero; **60-61** *tr* Still Pictures/Norbert Wu; **61** *tr* Still Pictures/Fritz Polking, *bl* www.osf.uk.com/John Brown, *br* Frank Lane Picture Agency/Minden Pictures; **62** *tr* Still Pictures/D. Decobecq, *cl* Corbis/Kevin Schafer; **62-63** *b* NHPA/Martin Harvey; **63** *tl* BBC Natural History Unit Picture Library/ John Cancalosi, *cr* www.osf.uk.com/Tui De Roy; **64** *tr* Still Pictures/Ronald Seitre, *cl* Still Pictures/ Ronald Seitre, *br* Still Pictures/Klein/Hubert; **65** *tl* Ardea London/Hans & Judy Beste, *cr* NHPA/ Ann & Steve Toon, *b* Ardea London/Jean-Paul Ferrero; **66** *tr* Clive Gifford, *bl* Getty Images; **66-67** *b* Still Pictures/Sarvottam Rajkoomar; **67** *tr* www.osf.uk.com/Victoria McCormick, *br* Corbis; **68** *tl* NHPA/Nigel J. Dennis, *tr* Ardea London/ Liz & Tony Bomford, *b* Ardea London/J. B. & S. Bottomley; **69** *tr* NHPA/Daniel Heuclin, *cl* NHPA/ John Buckingham, *br* Ardea London/Martin W. Grosnick; **70** *bl* Still Pictures/Mark Edwards; **70-71** Still Pictures/Ray Pfortner; **71** *tr* Corbis/ Michael S. Yamashita, *cl* Ardea London/ M. Watson, *br* Still Pictures/Pierre Gleizes; **72** *c* NHPA/Daryl Balfour, *bl* www.osf.uk.com/Olivier Grunewald; **73** *cl* Still Pictures/G. Griffiths/ Christian Aid, *br* NHPA/Alberto Nardi.

Key: b = bottom, c = center, l = left, r = right, t = top

Every effort has been made to trace the copyright holders of the photographs. The publishers apologize for any inconvenience caused.